Re-thinking Development in Africa: an Oral History Approach from Botoku, Rural Ghana

Komla Tsey

Langaa Research & Publishing CIG
Mankon, Bamenda

Publisher:
Langaa RPCIG
Langaa Research & Publishing Common Initiative Group
P.O. Box 902 Mankon
Bamenda
North West Region
Cameroon
Langaagrp@gmail.com
www.langaa-rpcig.net

Distributed in and outside N. America by African Books Collective
orders@africanbookscollective.com
www.africanbookcollective.com

ISBN: 9956-726-50-8

About the Author

Komla Tsey is a research professor of education for social sustainability at James Cook University's Cairns Institute in Australia. Komla has a broad research and teaching interest in the reasons why some people are healthy and others not, or what has been called the social determinants of health. He is also interested in the types of government policies and local community actions, and social and cultural values and expectations that can enable individuals, families and broader communities of people to achieve health and well-being.

Komla was born and educated in Ghana. After earning a BA honours degree from the University of Ghana in 1980, Komla studied for a PhD in Social Science (Economic History) at Glasgow University, Scotland, where his thesis examined the social, economic and health consequences of British colonial railway investments in Ghana. He returned to the University of Ghana where he lectured and developed partnerships with his rural communities as a participant observer, researching long-term development projects aimed at improving the availability and access to facilities such as schools, health services and water and sanitation. Since the 1990's, Komla has been living in Australia researching and learning about health and well-being, mainly with Aboriginal organizations and communities. He continues to undertake longitudinal studies of community development projects in Ghana. Komla has written more than 100 academic journal articles and research reports on a wide range of topics including: community development; traditional medicine; mental health; sex, alcohol and violence; needs analysis and resource allocation; education and health; participatory action research; empowerment; social and emotional well-being; and evaluation research. His forthcoming book, From Head Loading to the Iron Horse, tells the story of the unequal social and economic consequences of British colonial railway building in tropical Africa with particular focus on the Gold Coast, modern Ghana.

Intended Audience

This book is intended for NGOs and other international development agencies; government policy–makers; academic researchers and students of development studies; and local community development leaders. Most importantly, this book deliberately uses simple story telling approaches aimed at the lay person or general reader, both African and non-African, interested in understanding development in Africa.

Dedication

I dedicate this book to the people of Botoku in appreciation of the high value they have always placed on education and to my parents in particular for sacrificing the little they had in order to support my education.

Table of Contents

Chapter 1

Introduction

Why is it always Africa? What at all is wrong with Africa? Why is it that nothing good comes out of Africa? Any time you turn on the TV it is always bad news: hunger, massacre, war, military coup, greed, corruption, child labour, rape, tribalism, hero worship; you name it. What at all is wrong with Africa? - A Botoku diaspora resident in the UK reflecting on the African condition, April 2010

This book uses oral history to examine the concept of development, and the way the citizens of one particular rural Ghanaian community, Botoku, sought to achieve development and the challenges and opportunities they encountered over the years. By development, I refer to the individual and collective efforts taken by Botoku citizens, both residents and those living outside the area, to bring about improvements in the material, social, cultural and spiritual living conditions of the ancestral home.

Three factors motivated me to write this book. The first was simply to write a book about development in Africa that is accessible to the lay reader; rather than directed to the specialized development policy maker, researcher, or field practitioner alone. The number of books, academic articles and reports written over the last 60 years on how best to understand and foster development in Africa is staggering, to say the least. Unfortunately, these are all written in a manner and style appealing to development policy makers, academics, and the large army of development workers employed by non-government organizations, known as NGOs for short, and other international agencies worldwide. The lay person in Africa, usually the target of development goals, is totally removed from the development discourse. Similarly, development literature bypasses the large numbers of well meaning people living in advantaged countries, who are constantly bombarded by commercials encouraging donations towards development in Africa and other parts of the developing world. From the outset, the challenge I set myself was to write a book sophisticated enough to engage complex development concepts and methodologies, but at the same time straight forward enough to be accessible to a general readership.

In countless conversations with Africans, both living in Africa and abroad, I am always struck by the general sense of frustration, anger, shame, and even sense of hopelessness, about their own inability to make sense of the African condition. The questions from my focus group discussions with groups of Botoku people living in the UK (cited in the quotation at the beginning of this introduction) are typical of the widespread sense of frustration, and are worth mentioning again.

Why is it always Africa? What at all is wrong with Africa? Why is it that nothing good comes out of Africa? Any time you turn on the TV it is always hunger, massacre, war, military coup, greed, corruption, child labour, rape, tribalism, hero worship. What at all is wrong with Africa?

It is amazing the extent to which Africans are happy to ponder, and freely express their frustrations in conversations with fellow Africans, the difficulty of making sense of Africa's problems. These conversations though, never take place in the midst of those they consider outsiders or non-Africans.

For Africans in Africa, it is simply beyond their comprehension to imagine the huge differences between the extreme poverty that surrounds them and the relative comfort that exists in the West. Most sincerely believe however, that once they make it to the West, all will be fine. So a large majority of Africans who leave do so with the intention of getting education or skills, accumulating capital, all with the eventual intent of building a house back in their own country. Once they have achieved this they can return, having ensured a better life for themselves, and their children, and children's children. Of course, one thing leads to another and many never do return home and it becomes even more difficult for their children, and children's children, to return. What does development in Africa mean to these African diaspora (people living outside Africa)? Do they see a role for themselves, or their children, or children's children in that development? What do the brothers and sisters left in Africa think of this diaspora living in the affluent West? Do they perceive a role or responsibility for them in the development of their country and ancestral home? My hope, for Africans both living in Africa and outside of Africa, is that this book will provide a framework for them to make sense of the contemporary African situation. It is my hope they will come to understand the respective roles they may be able to play in contributing towards development.

My second reason for writing this book is to sort out and express the sense of frustration I have felt for a long time about the lack of a historical approach to understanding development. There is a tendency among those writing about development to take a short-term view; or a snapshot of their subject at a particular point in time. They use this as the example for focusing on a specific problem, project, or policy initiative over a short period, or at best a five-year period. Even for those with reasonably longer-term views, such as the current 15-year United Nations Millennium Development Goals (2011), the focus is still on monitoring and evaluating specific investment initiatives. Rarely do analysts take a broad historical view; a view that would help with understanding the evolution and changes in the complex and interconnected material, social, cultural and spiritual aspects of the human experience. This, in my view, is critical to fully understanding development. I understand that one reason for short-term goals is that development funding is dependent on the three to four year life cycles of democratically elected governments. This makes it hard for policy makers to commit public resources beyond the life of the existing government. Another reason for the existing short-term view is that development, as a discipline, has traditionally attracted economists, sociologists, anthropologists, geographers, engineers, agriculturalists and health and education practitioners, but unfortunately, not trained historians who might push for the bigger picture. I believe understanding the complexities of an elusive concept such as development requires no less than a long-term historical approach.

My final reason for writing this book is to help make sense of my recent appointment as research professor of education for social sustainability. In Australia, where I currently live and work, it has become national education policy (since 2008) that all schools and tertiary education courses explicitly weave three priority issues into the curriculum: Indigenous Australian knowledge systems; Asia and Australia's engagement with Asia; and concepts of sustainable living. The latter may be defined briefly as the notion that the current generation lives their lives in such a way that they do not disadvantage the lives of others within the present or future generations. Unlike the more tangible aspects of sustainability, such as environmental and economic sustainability, I find researchers and teachers struggling to define, let alone convey, the social dimensions of sustainability in their research and teaching. What is even more worrying is the tendency among researchers, with a focus on the environment or the economic dimensions of sustainability, to view the social aspects of sustainability as a vehicle to achieving their goals, rather than valuing social goals as legitimate ends in their own right. The point I am trying to make is best illustrated by a few statistics from documents such as the UN's report on human development. In a matter of twenty-five years, from 2000 to 2025, the global urban population, it is estimated, will double as a staggering 180,000 people are added every single day. As much as 95% of this urban growth will be in the less-developed world. In practical terms this means that every week, for the next 30 years or so, the equivalent of a new city with a population of one million people is needed to accommodate the doubling of the urban population in developing countries alone, from two billion to four billion (ARUP, 2008; UN Human Development Report, 2008).

The inequalities and associated tensions, anxieties and sometimes open conflicts over resources between and within cities and rural areas can be huge. For example, cities house half the world's population but consume three-quarters of the world's resources and produce three-quarters of the world's pollution. One-third of the world's urban population lives in what are defined by the UN as slum conditions (ARUP, 2008; UN Human Development Report, 2008). In the context of these global challenges, are there any potential opportunities for micro rural communities achieving sustainable livelihoods? Is small, idyllic, sparsely populated rural and remote dwelling a thing of the past? This is a global challenge for both wealthy nations and poorer countries. The extent and manifestation of the challenge may differ from place to place, but no matter which country, the capacity of rural populations to achieve healthy and sustainable livelihoods are under severe pressure everywhere (Ashley & Maxwell, 2001). This is particularly the case with minority indigenous populations living in wealthy nations like Australia, but it is also the case with many developing countries.

Yet politics or decisions about what is good and what is bad for society, which according to Aristotle and countless local indigenous knowledge traditions ought to be guided by practical wisdom, is today reduced to image driven opinion polls. The traditional role of the media as the fourth estate has been reduced to television ratings and unreflective presentation of both sides of the main political parties, without critical judgment as to what is good or bad for society. It is of little surprise that, despite all our scientific and technological advances, many people today, irrespective of whether they live in poor or rich countries, are confused as to our purpose in this life. For example, research on wellbeing, resiliency and happiness is increasingly focused on the concept of "flourishing" and has thereby illuminated an important aspect of the social problems of the 21st century. People who are flourishing are actively pursuing a happy life, have energy and skills to protect

4

their health, have higher productivity, less physical and mental illness and are more resilient. However, in USA, for example, only about 20% of adults were found to be flourishing despite material wealth (Keyes, 2005). Enabling this majority to flourish would be a tremendous opportunity to save costs to society from increased productivity as well as improved resiliency, health and wellbeing. In the contexts of current debates about climate change mitigation and adaptation that are marked by high degrees of complexity, uncertainty, and risks as to the best possible courses of action, approaches to learning that empower and enable the capacity of people to be more resilient, and hence agents of their own change, are bound to be at the core of education for sustainability more broadly and not just the social dimensions. Questions central to understanding social sustainability include: What levels of socio-economic inequalities are unavoidable, and even necessary, for example, as incentives for enterprise, innovation and hard work for a society that describes itself as civilized?

This book brings together the findings from longitudinal oral history research with my own community of Botoku to present a theoretical holistic model of development. As someone who has closely observed and participated in development activities in my native Botoku for close to 40 years, I believe Botoku has a story to share, not only about the sustainability of rural communities in the face of rapid rural to urban migration, but also the valuable contributions local indigenous knowledge systems can play towards sustainable livelihoods. It is a story from which most people, African or not, politician, development expert, academic, or the general reader, can learn about the material, social and spiritual dimensions of development.

A methodological challenge for this research is how one specific rural community worldview can have meaning for other African cultures beyond that of the specific? Why did I use a specific Botoku perspective rather than a pan-African approach? The unique aspects of African cultures, I believe, are valued because they emerge from long traditions of ancestral relationships and connections to particular homelands. These connections need to be acknowledged and respected. However, as Africans, we also share worldviews that hold common, enduring beliefs about the world. Though specific customs and protocols may vary, the underlying worldviews are not. It is my hope that this book will motivate other Africans to share their relevant local stories. The more we learn to listen to each others' stories the more we break down barriers and develop greater understanding of each other.

A reviewer commented on the manuscript that this book required patient reading. Understanding the teachings from the stories of Botoku or any other knowledge tradition does require patient listening. Yet it is from these local traditions that will be familiar to African people and from which they can hopefully build for their incremental and meaningful change.

This book is organized into eleven chapters, including this introduction. Chapter two uses a series of anecdotes to provide background information on Botoku (study context) as well as explains my relationship to the place. Chapter three describes the methodology, including the main sources of information for the book, and how I analysed or processed the information to make sense of the unfolding story. It also includes an overview of a conceptual framework for how this particular African community understands, experiences and talks about development. In chapter four the study participants draw upon their rich oral traditions, myths and legends, including ancient migratory stories. They remind us that the desire to have a better future for themselves and their children's children, which lies at the core of development, has always been integral to the history of Botoku. The importance of *afemenunya* or wisdom that comes from tradition in the quest for a better future or development is highlighted.

Chapters five and six present a selection of significant development initiatives in the recent history of Botoku, ranging from the construction of an 18 km dirt road in the 1930s (allowing motor vehicles to access the village for the first time); to a middle school in the 50's; through to potable water, clinic, electrification projects, and *fiasa* or 'palace' from the 70s to 2000s. In chapter seven, I shift my attention to the role of customs and traditions or culture in legitimizing citizen participation, whether resident or not, in development initiatives. In the context of Botoku, development is more than building physical infrastructure. Development here is also about examining our customs and traditions, such as witchcraft and sorcery and looking at the extent to which they may, or may not, be helping us achieve our basic needs as human beings. This will lead to the question of what can be done to improve that situation.

The focus of chapter eight is making a living through meaningful participation in economic activity. It argues that if governments, NGOs and development donor agencies are really serious about development, they need to get down to grass roots levels, both metaphorically and literally. They must search deep to develop meaningful understanding about those development activities that should fall within the legitimate domain of the public sphere, and those that fall under the private sphere. For those that are public, it is imperative that all citizens, both resident and non, contribute their fair share. For those deemed private, it must be understood they are best left to the individuals, family groups and private cooperatives directly involved. I argue that failure to make this distinction has been a major contributor to the failure of countless development initiatives in Africa.

For the Botoku people who participated in this study and their friends, development, or the quest for a better future, is also about having an ancestral home or place with which to connect. This connection may be physical as in a place to live and make a living. It may also be mental or spiritual, especially for those living away from the ancestral village. The variety of ways in which Botoku natives, and indeed most southern Ghanaians, seek to express connection to ancestral home is the focus of chapter nine. In chapter ten, the last substantive in the book, I bring together the key findings of the research as described in the various chapters of the book in order to build a theoretical model of development. At the center of the model is the way this particular community understands, experiences and describes development, in terms of past and present achievements, difficulties and lessons learned along the way, and the desire for a better future for themselves, their children and grandchildren. The desire for a better future encompasses not only material elements but also the social, cultural and spiritual aspects of life. Underpinning all these was *afemenunya,* or wisdom that comes from tradition, manifesting as sets of personal virtues, values, beliefs and attitudes they believe are vitally important in any efforts to achieve a better future. These are qualities they believed development should ultimately be about.

The concluding chapter briefly summarizes key messages from the book. The hope is to highlight the importance of combining local traditional knowledge systems, with social scientific approaches and evidence, to support micro communities in their efforts to achieve a better future.

The story that emerges from this book is one based on strength, hope, resiliency, and a positive and future orientation to life, entirely different from the problem-saturated or bad news stories we are so used to about Africa. Because I wanted this story to be accessible as much to the general reader as to the academic audience, I decided not to cloud or litter the pages of this book with too many references and footnotes as is often expected of academic writing. What I have done instead is to cite as few sources as possible in the text mainly those to which I make direct references. Other sources relevant to the ideas in the book are included as bibliography.

This introduction will not be complete without expressing my deep appreciation and gratitude to my families, colleagues and friends, too many to mention each individually by name. Your encouragement and support made it possible for me to write this book. The list that follows represents only a tiny proportion of many of you who have been behind the scene. I am grateful to you all for your contributions and as the Botoku people say *akpe kakaka loo* (thank you very much)! To Annie my wife and my children Kwame, Sena, Kafui, Amenyo and Novi, I say thank you for your love, support and putting up with what my friends and families often describe as my "weird" working hours. I thank the late *Togbe Tamtia V* and the chiefs and elders and all those of you Botoku people and their friends who gave your time and information towards this book. *Togbega,* I still remember your words of appreciation and encouragement to me in 1997 to keep writing about Botoku and to make sure that whatever name I called this book Botoku appeared in it. Fo Kwesi Asemda, you took your role as research assistant very seriously and I say thank you for competently documenting some of the stories in my absence. I thank Colonel Asamoah for his collaborative history project with me from which I also draw for this book. My thanks also go to: Ayoyo, Victor Abotsi, Foster Dankwa and Seth from Botoku; Janya, Roxanne, Cath, Olivia, Yvonne, Annita, Katrina, Elena, Mandy, Snowy, Michelle, Bob and other colleagues and friends at The Cairns Institute and JCU; Astri and Sarah, Mary, Annekathrin, Radhika, Melissa, Crystal, Heather Kirk (Happy Marketing) for editing the manuscript; and Australian National Health and Medical Council for fellowship support during part of this research.

Chapter 2

Better Understanding Botoku and My Connection to It

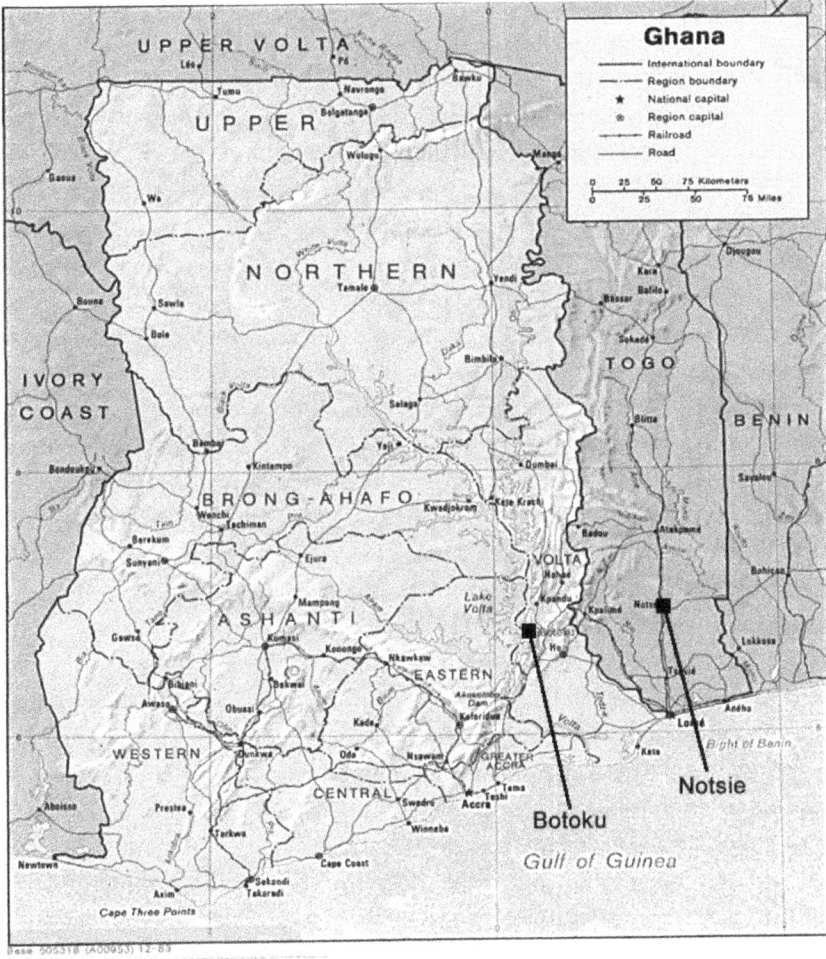

Botoku is a large rural community located in the Kpandu District in southeastern Ghana, 200km from the capital Accra.

Set in a valley and surrounded by a range of hills, Botoku is bordered by the Volta Lake in the west, the River Dayi in the east and neighboring villages of Tsrukpe and Tsoxor in the north and south respectively. Botoku also shares a boundary with the people of Wusuta in the northwest. Like most parts of

9

rural Ghana, population estimates are notoriously unreliable; however estimates set the population at about 10,000 people. Of these, about 3,000 are residents in Botoku, while the larger majority live and work in the urban centers and other parts of Ghana and beyond. These residents are classified as *dutanolawo,* meaning those living in other people's homes, or non-resident citizens. For Botuku people, a citizen is defined broadly to include anyone with ancestral links to the village, irrespective of where they are born or live.

This concept of an extended community might be best illustrated by examples. A person originally from Botoku leaves the country to settle in the U.S. They raise a family and then one day one of their children gives them a grandchild. This child may never visit Ghana, let alone the Botoku ancestral village in their life, may never identify with the Botoku people or participate in any of their ways or traditions, yet, as far as the Botoku people are concerned, this child is a Botoku citizen and will be treated as such.

While people with ancestral ties to the community are welcomed instantly, not all who actually live in the community are considered residents. People with no ancestral ties to the village, even when they reside there, become residents by virtue of long-term residence. They must be long-term residents specifically, and they must be adopted into one of the clan groups, rather than simply making it their current place of residence.

Of particular interest to me is the role non-resident Botoku citizens play in initiating and contributing towards development projects back in the village. I am also interested in the role culture (defined here as customs and traditions) plays in legitimizing and sustaining both resident and non-resident participation in village development.

Statistical profiles on rural communities in Ghana, such as Botoku, are notoriously unreliable. I have therefore decided to use an anecdote surrounding a primary school group photo taken in 1964 to give the reader a feel for the demographic context, instead of limiting myself to using numerical or statistical numbers alone. Realistically numbers rarely have any resemblance to the real life situation, and in the case of these rural communities, even less so.

In 2005, an Australian friend asked me whether my child, a toddler at the time, resembled me when I was a child. I really didn't know. We had a planned trip to Ghana a few months away so I decided to satisfy our curiosity and resolved I would ask my elder sisters and other family members. The friend looked puzzled when I explained my plan and said, "Why don't you bring your baby photos to show me so we can see? Why do you have to wait to ask your sister?" My wife (New Zealand born) responded that she was just realizing she had never seen any childhood photos of me. It struck me then that until I left Ghana to do graduate studies in Glasgow in my late 20's I had never been in a photo except in passport sized photos for official purposes. These required photos would have been used for secondary school admission exams; sixth form exams; my first job as civil servant; university entrance exams; and a passport to travel outside Ghana. After pondering the issue for a while I recalled an incident, in primary four in Botoku, when our class teacher, Miss Boge, organized a group photo for us and everyone paid to get a copy. She was leaving us at the end of the school year to go to teachers' college and wanted photos of us to remind her of her stay in Botoku. I remembered that termites had destroyed my photo, together with the few old exercise books I had, only a few years after the photo was taken. But I was convinced some of my classmates back in Ghana would certainly have copies of the photo. Thus, when we visited Ghana two months later, I began my wild goose chase tracking down the elusive photo. The first person I asked in the village had the same termite story as I but referred me to someone else they thought might have fared better. Sadly, the first six people I contacted, all still living in the village, had similar stories: eaten by termites; lost; can't remember where I kept it; or, I gave it to my mother to keep and when she died I couldn't locate it. One close friend in particular took up my quest to find a copy of the photo. He found the mobile phone numbers of two of our friends living in Accra and referred me to them, believing both were the most organized in our class and the most likely to still have the photo I sought. Unfortunately, neither they, nor other people I contacted from outside the village, could seem to locate the photo I was now obsessed with finding. For some strange reason, the more people I asked and the more people couldn't help, the more determined I became to get hold of the photo. I suppose my interest was partly because everyone I had asked was now also excited about the prospect of seeing how we looked more than 40 years ago. Convinced I would eventually find it, everyone had made requests for copies once, not if, I tracked it down. After four visits to Ghana over four years, I succeeded in locating Miss Boge, who was by then a retired school teacher in her village. On my first visit to her village I met with her mother, a lady probably in her 80's, but still in good health. Miss Boge was away visiting family but her mother offered to contact her, with the help of my mobile phone, which she used to make the call. The call went through and a voice I remember distinctly came on the line. Fortunately she

11

remembered me, and several of my classmates, among them Gbordzoe and Anka. After catching up for a bit on who was where – Gbordzoe was in the U.S. and Anka had died long ago - I asked about the photo and she assured me she still had it. She was returning to the village in about three days' time and suggested I call on her to collect it then. Though that was the day I was leaving for Accra to fly back to Australia I decided to visit early in the morning and collect the photo on my way. Miss Boge was obviously very happy and proud to hear one of her star pupils had become a university professor in Australia and was keen to show me off to all her neighbours so they could see the fruits of her labour. She was sad to tell me though, she had just returned from Accra late the previous night, very tired and had been unable to find the photo where she thought it would be. She offered to take my nephew's phone number and said she would call as soon as she was able to locate it. I was very disappointed and thought it was just a continuation of the wild goose chase I had been on with my classmates, but thanked her for her offer. Three months later my nephew called me in Australia to say Miss Boge had given him the photo and he was sending it registered delivery to me. After an anxious three-week wait the parcel arrived, and there was the photo: a diminutive black and white piece showing two teachers and 42 children (22 boys and 20 girls) crammed into it.

Eagerly armed with reading glasses and the lid from a bug catcher borrowed from my children to aid magnification, I pored over it for hours chuckling away to myself as I recognized my mates. Anyway, I made several enlargements and passed them along to all the friends I had become reacquainted with along the way. I had one made for Miss Boge as well so she had a copy that was more visible.

My reason for telling this anecdote, besides illustrating the challenges of capturing and documenting life in Botoku, is the reference to Anka's death. We, as children, were very close friends. As I examined the photo carefully, I glimpsed a microcosm of a Botoku demographic profile. There appeared to be a large prevalence of preventable deaths, especially among the boys who had migrated away from the village in search of better opportunities in the cities and other parts of the country. Of the 42 pupils in the photo, one had died before the class completed elementary school and another shortly thereafter. By the time we were in our forties as many as ten or 24% of our classmates had passed away. Nine of the 10 deaths (90%) were males who, with the exception of one person, all lived outside the village at the time of their deaths. It is not possible to be definitive about the causes of these deaths but anecdotal evidence suggests preventable factors such as accidents, hernia due to heavy lifting, cardiovascular problems, malaria complications commonly known as *asra* or fever, and at least one suspected case of HIV/AIDS. Of the 32 still alive, 15 or 47% still live in the village. They consisted of 12 females (80%) and three males (20%).

The other striking thing about the photo was the unbelievable levels of social stratification and the associated huge income disparities and unequal life chances, totally unbeknown to most of our parents' generation, created through the availability of universal primary school education in a matter of a single generation. Of the original 42 pupils, only three (7%), all boys, gained secondary school education, while several boys and girls went on to a range of technical and vocational colleges and trade apprentices. Of the three who went to high school, only one resides in Ghana and is a university academic in agricultural science; one is a computer programmer in the US; and then there is myself in Australia. A female pupil in the photo, described by my friend as one of the two most organized among us, did not go to secondary school or other post elementary training because, like the majority of the class, there was no financial support and she had not secured a scholarship which would have allowed her to go. Interestingly, this girl went on to become a trader in textiles and very successful. Starting with table-top selling

13

of a few pieces of print materials, over the years she became one of the prominent female traders of Accra, popularly known as Makola Market Queens, noted for their power to bring down governments by creating artificial shortages of essential goods. For her, success seems destined, whether she was formally educated beyond the elementary school level or not. Of the others, some found their niche in white collar employment such as teaching, while others entered a variety of technical and commercial trades. At the other end of the income distribution spectrum however are several former mates who are living in relative poverty, either as subsistence farmers in the village, or trying to eke out a living elsewhere in the urban sprawls of Ghana.

The contradictory nature of education, especially in transitional post colonial societies such as Ghana which are embarking on major social reforms, including universal education as described in this anecdote, resonate powerfully with the UN Human Development Report (2010) findings. On the positive side the report highlighted remarkable achievements by many African countries, including Ghana, in expanding education and primary health care facilities since independence. The average life expectancy for people in Ghana is 57.1 years, almost five years above the average for Sub-Saharan Africa. The mean years of schooling is 7.1, well over the 4.5 average for the whole region and relatively close to the expected 9.7 years of schooling the report suggests a country like Ghana will attain. Despite these advances material poverty remains a major barrier to prosperity and well-being, as evident by Ghana's GIP per capita of $1,385 compared with the average of $37,225 for developed countries such as Australia (UN Human Development Report, 2010). Importantly, the same educational opportunities are also, in many ways, contributing to a growing income gap between the haves and the have not's on a scale previously unknown, not only across broader society, but within family groups. The challenges of negotiating such socio-economic disparities at personal, family and broader community levels, especially in the context of a cultural belief that whatever belongs to one person belongs to the whole extended family, and indeed the entire community, are addressed in this book.

At this point it is important I say a bit more about myself; how I became involved in community development related activities some 40 years ago and how those early formative influences continue to inform my research and development work to this day. I will start with two of my favourite anecdotes. The first happened in 1970 when I left the Botoku village to attend boarding school in a nearby town. On one of my holidays back in the village, my father struck up a conversation with me about the relevance of what we were learning at school to the needs of our village. I was glad my father showed an interest but I found myself struggling to relate my studies to anything concrete to answer his question directly. After a period of silence my father looked into my eyes and said, "Look, our child, if we send you to boarding school and you cannot come back to this village and find ways of explaining and making what you are learning at the school relevant to the interests and aspirations of people in this village, then what is the point of you going to school? The more you make your learning relevant to your people, the stronger you become in who you are, no matter where you go."

The other incident occurred several years later when as an undergraduate student in the 70's I approached the chiefs and elders of Botoku for permission to research the impact the Volta hydroelectric project of the 1960s was having on the people of Botoku. My real agenda was to use the study as a way of raising awareness of the huge social, economic and environmental consequences the artificially created lake was having, especially for communities in the immediate vicinity. In the ensuing discussions, the chiefs and elders convinced me that if I was going to do a study on the village, their priority was for me to start by recording the largely oral traditions and history of the village itself. Their argument was simple: with education, Christianity and modernization, few young people had the opportunity to participate in the avenues of transmitting traditions, such as during festivals, sacred drums and songs, oaths and appellations. They believed that in keeping with the changing circumstances, we should start using the relatively new technology of writing to record the history of the village. I agreed to the suggestion and, obviously, the chiefs and elders were pleased that for the first time, the predominantly oral accounts of the village would be written.

After meticulous preparation with my research methods lecturer at the university, I selected information-rich people for interviews using semi-structured questions. After a few scheduled interviewees failed to materialize due to a range of excuses, some questionable in my mind, I approached one of the respected elders, a distant uncle, in frustration. In a calming voice he said to me that he thought I was going about my study the wrong way. He reminded me that Botoku people had always had their own ways of telling stories or transmitting history. He asked me to think carefully about *ekododo* or the procedure for narrating genealogical accounts. He said the steps were the same as the procedure for consulting *abrewa* (mythical wise old lady reputed for her wisdom) during conflict mediation (Chapter Seven). The best way to proceed, he believed, was for me to start with group, rather than one-on-one discussions, since it was the approach the people knew best. Once they became comfortable with working with me as a group, then of course, they would guide me to the individuals who were knowledgeable about particular stories. At that point they would also be happy for me to share with them my ways of doing things, as I was learning from university.

Although I found it difficult to make the connection between *ekododo* or *abrewa gbo* and the interviews I was going to do, it soon became clear the key steps necessary to get to the *yatia* (essence of the story) my elderly uncle was trying to tell me, had a lot in common with the steps involved in gathering and analyzing various types of qualitative research data. The three-step process can be described as follows: 1) give everyone the opportunity to have a say if they so wish; 2) negotiate a consensus position which allows scope for disagreements and contradictions to be accommodated within the same story line; and 3) the *tsiami* or spokesperson models and conveys the right story convincingly. I discovered that, unlike the conventional qualitative research where the researcher collects all the information and then single handedly analyzes and produces findings, with the *eko dodo* or *abrewa gbo* approach, half the analysis is done for you by the research participants themselves. This is because of the emphasis placed on mediation and negotiation of conflicting views and perspectives as potentially different interpretations of the same events and hence willingness to accommodate such diversity as part of broader storylines.

These and similar formative incidents, and my subsequent reflections on them, led me to a lifetime of involvement in community development and related social research. Since then, I have played a wide range of roles: as letter writer, translator, interpreter and advisor, for the chiefs and elders of my village, regarding development issues. I have held executive positions in development associations, and positions as an academic researcher, trainer and facilitator, using mainly action research strategies. In all of these roles, the two interrelated questions I keep asking myself are: what are the *interests and aspirations* of the people with whom I work and, how can I make my knowledge, skills and experience *relevant* to those interests and aspirations? Through this and other more formal community development processes I developed the understanding that, no matter how desperate the social conditions of a community of people might look to the outsider, there are always pockets of strength, resiliency and creativity within such communities and it is the role of the development facilitator to locate and work with such centers of strength and energy. This led me to the use of strengths-based facilitation approaches to engage and tap into peoples' own cultural resources as strengths, rather than simply targeting deficits, thereby inspiring confidence and hope, that no matter how desperate a social problem might look, there are always possibilities for using such problems as opportunities to change things for the better.

This approach, which sits at the core of all of my work, makes it extremely relevant and adaptable across different cultures and for addressing different types of education, health and well-being issues in areas such as rural Ghana, Aboriginal Australia and Papua New Guinea. I have learned the valuable lesson that community development is more than building physical infrastructure. Central to community development is the capacity to confront and, sensitively but firmly, deal with customs and traditions deeply rooted in unequal power relationships. These are generally contrary to health and well-being, or violate sections of the community's basic human rights and dignities. This is particularly the case among traditionally-oriented societies experiencing rapid social change. The community development practitioner is routinely confronted with issues such as the role and position of women and children in society, child brides, violence and abuse, substance abuse, sorcery and witchcraft; all of which have profound effects on health and well-being.

I have experienced the importance of narrative, or the human propensity to share stories of human diversity, as fundamental to working with people, especially when tackling difficult and sensitive cultural beliefs and attitudes. I have developed facilitation approaches that seek to create safe environments for critical dialogue to occur between diverse groups with unequal positions of power and influence.

One of my very satisfying formative roles was that of letter writer, where I drafted all sorts of letters, both official and private. The letters that had the most lasting impression on me were the private letters I wrote, mainly for women and their children left behind in the village by their husbands or fiancées. These men had gone to urban centers, cocoa farms or the mines in search of employment and education opportunities. The 1960s was a period of rapid social change, including rural-urban migration. This was due to a combination of post independence euphoria (Ghana gained independence from the British in 1957), the long post war economic boom, significant expansion in primary school education, and to a limited extent, secondary schools. For towns and villages such as Botoku, in the immediate vicinity of the largest artificially created lake in the world, the inundation of the lake on traditional farming and hunting lands became additional push factors, literally driving thousands of young people from their rural communities to urban areas.

In Southern African mining towns at the time, black migrant workers were prevented by law from bringing their families, and instead had to live in adult male dormitories. In contrast, men, and indeed anybody, migrating from rural areas to the towns and cities, were free to take their families with them; but there was a catch. To bring a family to the city one needed to have the money to be able to rent a room in the large, privately owned, compound house often with limited, if any, sanitation and other shared amenities. Most migrants would start off by lodging with families or friends, with an understanding that once they secured a job they would save enough to be able to pay a deposit on a room of their own and then they could bring their families to join them. In the sprawling urban slums, where demand for housing stock always outstrips supply, landlords could demand anything from one to three year's worth of rent as a deposit. A man leaving the village with the intent of having his family join him may take a long while to raise the money needed to send for his family, if it happened at all.

Taking up my father's advice to make my learning relevant to my people, particularly with regards to these women and children left behind in the village, I, and other school children like myself, became the main conduit of communication between the people migrating away from the village and the families they left behind. Every now and then a letter would arrive in the village, either delivered through a Botoku person visiting home from the urban centers or, less frequently, via the post. A typical letter from the men would start by asking how everybody was. It would say whether they had gotten a job or not; provide update on efforts to get enough deposit to rent a room; ask about everybody at home… It would then end by saying when they hope to visit home next or send for the family to come and join them. I would read the letter to the woman, who in turn would dictate her reply to me to record and send to her man. Typically, the woman would tell him how everybody was doing at home; whether any of the children had been sick; about any deaths that occurred in the village, along with an inquiry as to whether he would be coming for the funeral; reminders of the children's school fees; how hard it was to make ends meet; thanks for any money sent with the letter; reminders to send money for fish, salt and kerosene for the lamp (things that no peasant farmer could produce by themselves).

As a child, I loved the Ghanaian-Ananse folk-lore. They were epic stories with the spider, reputed for its cleverness, as the main character. Unlike the Ananse stories that surrounded every Ghanaian child at the time, full of intrigue, love, passion, determination, loyalty and so on, I found the letters I was reading from the men to the women and those the women were dictating to me to write so dry. They were matter of fact about practical things in every way and totally lacking in passion, sentiment and affection. It is of course, not right in many places for people to express affection or romantic love openly but I was young and thought these letters should be so much more. So, based upon my love of Ananse stories, I began spicing up the letters the women were dictating to me a little bit at a time. For instance I might end the letters with 'mele susuo kakaka,' meaning 'I am missing you very much!' Every letter I wrote I had to read back to the woman to ensure I got what she was saying right. When I got to the end of the letter where I had ad-libbed, all the women said, with pleasant surprise was, "You cheeky boy Komla, did I ask you to write that?" None of them ever asked me to cross it out. On the contrary, I sensed they enjoyed it and, with time, started dictating on their own the same kinds of things to write. But, what amazed me most was when the men too started ending their letters with the same or similar expressions. The women would often ask me with surprise, "Did he really say that? Read it again."

As I reflected years later on this, and similar formative experiences, as part of grappling with the perennial problems about the nature of change, specifically how to bring about social and behavior change in efforts to achieve development or improve the human condition, I could not help but sympathize with complexity theorists. The idea being that in any complex interconnected social system, if you can get one element working or behaving differently in a desired direction, the chances are that, with time, other constituent parts of the system may start following suit or behaving in a similar fashion. This is why the process of change, in many ways, can be likened to the rippling effects that results from dropping a pebble in water, or as the Australian singer Kev Carmody put it poetically in his song 'from little things big things grow.' In other words, bringing about change in any social situation can be hard, but not necessarily impossible.

Though such early experiences were wonderful opportunities for me, of course, not every village school child would have the opportunity to be a village letter writer. Indeed today, mobile phones, rather than letters, are the main way people in the village communicate with their families living elsewhere.

The point I am trying to make here is that, for children who are not from middle class backgrounds, where going to school is not automatically accepted as what every child does, I see opportunities for schools and parents to work together to find creative ways to value and reward children for the skills they acquire at school. And that is the key: creative ways that use the traditions, cultural dynamics and needs of the community. Even for middle class children, acknowledging that, as a society, we value the knowledge and skills they are acquiring at school, no matter the level, can be good for the child's confidence, identity and sense of purpose. Imagine the power of that message where there may not be other supports and forms of encouragement.

Looking at the bigger picture, if the purpose of education is not just to get jobs but also to contribute to improving the human condition generally, then the different ways in which children's knowledge and expertise can be harnessed towards improving the human condition is endless. These are issues addressed in the context of sustainable development towards the end of this book. Presently, I will shift my attention in the next chapter to explain how I sought to gather and process the information for the book.

Chapter 3

My Approach to the Research

There are two main things I wish to cover in this chapter, and will illustrate these by recounting some of the main challenges and opportunities I encountered in trying to document the recent history of community development in Botoku. The main point I wish to highlight is the role valuable local indigenous knowledge systems can play in promoting unique understandings about sustainable development and how local communities might go about achieving the same. But for researchers to fully appreciate and maximize the potential of these local knowledge bases in assisting their research, they will need to develop patience and a high capacity for deep-listening. The second thing to highlight is how I applied the principles of the local *eko dodo* (the framework for moderating genealogical narrative accounts) into this research.

This chapter represents one of the most surprising of all of the findings of the oral history project, from my point of view as researcher. No matter how long my experience in trying to apply local indigenous knowledge traditions in social research, I still feel a novice as I continue to learn new things and develop novel insights with each new project. My original intention was to ask my participants to reflect on community development projects such as schools, the health clinic, behaviour modification programs such as HIV and AIDS education, clean water, rural electrification, et cetera et cetera, in the recent history of the village. The idea behind this being, the more people reflect on their previous experiences about these projects, the more they are likely to learn from them. This is important for motivating and guiding future initiatives. In community development, where the process is slow and often takes a long time to achieve tangible results, this becomes increasingly crucial. Providing people with the opportunity to routinely reflect on how they are doing; what is working, what is not working; who is benefiting and who is missing out, and what needs to happen to improve the situation, is one way community development participants provide and receive critical feedback. Through this sharing, they come to appreciate the tiny incremental changes they may be making, even though the magnitude of the changes may be so small they are not initially or readily obvious. Little did

I know that writing the history of recent community development projects would lead me on an epic journey.

My journey took me through the origins, migratory stories and legends of Botoku people, from Notsie in present day Togo, to their first settlement in present Botoku some 300-400 years ago. I learned of their encounters, both peaceful and violent, with their Akan-speaking neighbours across the Volta River (now Lake). And I discovered the social, economic, political and spiritual transformations and changes that were brought about by German, and later British colonial rules, from the late 19th century through to Ghana becoming an independent country in the 1950's.

The methods for the current project, which occurred over a 15-year period between 1995 and 2010, involved semi-structured group discussions among Botoku citizens and their friends and associates, both residents and non-residents. In all, approximately 300 people participated. Participants in the groups were carefully recruited to reflect the changing demographic profile of the village. Included in the groups were male and female chiefs and their elders; resident and non-resident citizens; development project executives; project participants; school children and other young people; and church groups. Participants in the groups were asked to identify and narrate the histories of key community development initiatives in the recent history of the village, using these simple semi-structured questions as prompts:

- What in your view were the significant community development initiatives in Botoku's recent history?
- Can you tell me their stories!
- What were the main challenges and opportunities involved in undertaking these initiatives?
- What in your view is the future of rural communities such as Botoku?

The actual process of gathering and processing the data was based on the structured but flexible local *eko dodo* or *abrewa gbo* oral traditions of arriving at consensus with regards to historical events and other decision-making processes that are characterized by lack of consensus and conflicting views and perspectives. The aims of the project were explained to one group of people. A lengthy discussion of what people thought were the most important development initiatives occurred within the group. A *tsiami* or spokesperson was then appointed to narrate the story, while others interjected to make "corrections" as required. I then took the consensus

22

story to the next group who discussed the version of the story as narrated to them, made their own changes as they considered appropriate, and then appointed their own *tsiami* to narrate what, in their view, was the correct story. The process continued until new groups began accepting the narrative accounts as mainly correct, without many new changes and additions. At this stage I shifted my attention to other emergent storylines and the process repeated all over again with each new theme or storyline. The iterative process, as will become clearer through the subsequent chapters of this book, provided inbuilt capacity for multiple versions of the same account to be negotiated and accepted as valid interpretations. The successful application of this, in this rural Ghanaian context, confirms what analysts have long recognized: that narrative, or the process of sharing stories, breaks down barriers and misunderstandings, builds social cohesion and promotes community resilience and well-being (Bruner, 1990).

Most of the field work for the project occurred at Botoku, Accra and other major regional and district Ghanaian towns, where Botoku citizens reside in significant numbers. I also took advantage of overseas conferences and other travels to collect valuable information from Botoku citizens residing in the United Kingdom and elsewhere, in order to capture the unique international diaspora perspective. All the stories were collected largely in Ewe (Botoku language) and translated into English. I then spent considerable amounts of time sorting out the massive information before me into several broad themes, each comprising a multiplicity of constituent stories, before weaving them into the various storylines documented throughout the book. Development meetings and other community gatherings provided valuable opportunities for me to routinely narrate aspects of the research findings, both to authenticate the unfolding stories as well as trigger new ones. As a participant in and close observer of the Botoku development scene over the past 40 years, I also drew upon my own experiences and anecdotes as valuable and legitimate sources of information to complement and enrich the research participants' stories.

Two closely related challenges confronted me as researcher when I started the current study. There was an obvious tension, or mismatch, between my immediate interest in documenting the stories of recent community development projects, and an apparent lack of interest among the chiefs and elders to discuss any such issues, preferring to talk instead about the migratory stories of their ancestors and their subsequent encounters with their Akan-speaking neighbours across the Volta. Since these groups of people represented the most knowledgeable or information rich resource, and hence those I planned to interview first, there were challenges from the start. Drawing on what I believe was my tested flexible but outcome-oriented, facilitation expertise, I tried in vain, to steer the chiefs and elders away from migratory stories and Ashanti wars to a discourse about schools, roads and clinics. The second challenge lay in the responsibility I was about to undertake. As one of the first people entrusted to write down the largely oral histories of Botoku for the first time, I had always dreaded being regarded as the sole authority on these histories and traditions. As the Ewe saying goes, *agbale meble ameo*, which literally translates as 'a book does not lie.' Unlike oral accounts that can easily be manipulated, in societies where the tradition of writing is a recent phenomenon, people sincerely believe once something is written down in black and white, it is the gospel truth. This is a responsibility I had always approached with some trepidation or cautiousness. I was acutely aware different people wanted a written history of the village for different reasons. For some, there is a genuine belief a written story will preserve the histories and traditions of the village for posterity in the face of rapid social change. For others, a written history was simply an opportunity, at long last, to lay their hands on the incontrovertible truth; that truth to be used, not for any great design, but as a source of information to settle old scores around land disputes and litigation over chieftaincy successions.

My attempts to explain that whatever history I wrote would only be one version (among many others yet to come), as told by them and understood by me, did not go down well at all. What they wanted written was the "absolute truth" (*yantefe ntonto*) from which all Botoku people, both those at home and outside, and their children's children, could learn.

Anyone who has ever tried to record oral histories among similar communities knows very well that peoples' ability to locate events in historical time can be extremely limited. While I was busy scanning archival and other secondary written sources for dates, in the hope it would assist my participants in assigning estimated dates to their own accounts of events, I was clearly the only one with such concerns. My informants appeared concerned, not so much about when these events took place, but rather the meanings and interpretations different people assigned to the events.

How could I write an absolute truth applicable to all Botoku people at all places and at all times? In frustration, I asked what migration from Notsie and Ashanti wars had to do with community development in Botoku. I had already documented aspects of these stories as part of my undergraduate studies and the same chiefs and elders had since commissioned another Botoku person (a lawyer and historian recently retired as a colonel from the army) and me to write an official Botoku history, which we were still researching. I wanted to be careful the elders were not confusing the community development project with that of the official history. After considerable deliberation among the elders participating in the formative discussions, the *tsiami*, or spokesperson, provided, at length, my answer. Community development, to this group, meant a better future for them and their children's children. How could they talk about a better future if people did not know who they were as people? A better future for them was like a tree. You would never see the roots unless you were prepared to dig deeper and deeper. Looking just at what is in front of you, you only see the stem, the branches and the leaves, forgetting, or not understanding, that everything comes from the roots. A better future for them included knowing where they came from as people, where they are today and where they are going tomorrow. The search for a better future, it was explained, was the main reason their ancestors risked their lives to escape, under the cover of darkness, the tyrannical rule of the notorious King Agorkoli from the walled-city of Notsie, a very long time ago. The importance is not necessarily when or how these things happened, but what the stories say to us today about the kind of people our ancestors were and the types of *afemenunya* or wisdom that come from traditions that helped, or did not help them, in their search for a better future.

This conversation marked a turning point for me in my trepidation, or reluctance, to become custodian or arbiter over a written history most people believed was going to be the "absolute truth." I was pleasantly surprised my informants were trying to help me appreciate, not so much the historical accuracies of the particular events by themselves (this is almost impossible in most cases even with the best archival and other secondary sources), but rather sets of personal virtues, values, beliefs and attitudes they believe are essential in any efforts to achieve a better future. It was these qualities they believed development should ultimately be about. I listened carefully to the narratives, especially those from the chiefs and elders, and identified some consistently recurring words and expressions. As the custodians responsible for transmitting the customs and traditions from generation to generation, that these were of particular value to them and hence were highlighted in the stories, held merit. These expressions included phrases such as freedom from servitude, sacrifice for the love of your people, endurance, loyalty and perseverance. They included concepts like openness to new ideas, being prepared to change in line with changing circumstances and mechanisms to take in and integrate outsiders not of blood lineage into the body politic. Carefully woven through the stories are thought-provoking often humorous proverbs and sayings designed to bring home the morale of the stories being told. Thus, *edo me wuame wo todzo texo o*, literally means that no matter how hungry you are it makes no sense to set fire and roast your entire yam barn for a meal. The significance of this saying as far as development is concerned is that as humans we should not confuse the things that we *desire or want* materially, or otherwise, in life with the things that we actually *need* to be happy and fulfilled. Another saying, *ametsitsi meyoo nkume o, nlokpui me wo yona*, literally translates to: an elderly person (hence presumably wise) does not frown their face, rather it is the anus that is frowned. The significance in the context of development leadership is that, as a person to whom others may look up to in society, it is important to have the capacity to maintain balance, modesty, dignity, composure, and patience, even in the face of obvious provocation.

As I studied the narratives it also became obvious to me that, given the widespread and pervasiveness of slavery in the history of West Africa, a micro study of development in villages or towns similar to Botoku would not be complete without delving into this history and the ways in which it continues to shape contemporary events. What follows, in the next chapter, is therefore not so much an attempt to write an accurate historical account of Botoku's migratory and subsequent histories. Rather, my purpose is to present, as accurately as possible, summaries of selected narratives to illustrate some of the core values, beliefs and attitudes my research participants believe are essential to their perennial quest for a better future. My interest is in the meanings and significance these people attach to the historical events, rather than the factual accuracies of the events themselves. It is the morale or the lessons we can learn from the stories that are most important to my analysis.

Once I accepted the fact that for Botoku people, their ancient migratory and settlement stories are a necessary and legitimate starting point for any efforts to understand development, which in their view means a better future for them and their children's children, other things, not surprisingly, began falling into place. Those participating in the group discussions, both at Botoku and outside, felt much more comfortable to identify and tell the stories of what they believed were the most important development initiatives in the recent history of the village.

After presenting the migratory and settlement accounts in the next chapter, I then present the emergent themes in the form of a series of stories in the subsequent chapters.

Chapter 4

From Migration to Settlement

According to oral tradition, the people of present day Botoku, like those of all other Ewes, appear to have evolved, or at least once lived, somewhere in the Nile Valley, in north-eastern parts of Africa, some thousands of years before the birth of Christ. From this original cradle in the Nile Valley, several centuries of waves of migrations brought the Ewes in a south-westerly direction, until they came to live in a valley somewhere in the Niger Delta, now Nigeria. From here, the people moved down to Ketu, now the Republic of Benin, and then finally settled for a considerable length of time at Notsie, now the Republic of Togo. The Notsie settlement occurred around the 16th century (Lawrance, 2005).

Notsie was a large walled city with isolated farming settlements outside its walls. The fortified town provided sanctuary to the citizens in times of war and during slave raids. The relics of the heavily built walls, measuring four to eight metres in width, can still be seen at Notsie. The highest political authority in Notsie at the time was a divine monarch whose absolute powers, like those of all feudal chieftains of the time, were deeply rooted in stringent taboos. For example, it was forbidden to see the king, who went out of the palace only at night. Anyone who came across his path was instantly beheaded. The Notsie settlement also occurred at a time when the more established and powerful political entities raided and took members of smaller, and hence more vulnerable family groups and communities, as captives. These captives were deployed as domestic slaves by their captors, or sold to slave merchants to be exported to the Arab North Africa and the Middle East, the Americas and the Caribbean (Perbi, 2007).

The most vividly remembered of all the Notsie rulers was the one called King Agorkoli – sometimes known as Agokoli the Tyrant. He was reputed to be a very wicked and ruthless ruler who exacted harsh tolls from his people. As a result of his heavy handedness, all the citizens conspired and ran away, in small numbers at a time, usually under the cover of darkness, through escape exits they had secretly made in the fortified city walls. Subsequent waves of migration, and constant subdivisions of the units on a kinship basis, eventually led to the emergence of some 130 small autonomous political units or *dukowo* (towns and villages), which now occupy parts of the Volta

29

Region of Ghana and parts of the Republics of Togo and Benin. This ended a difficult and adventurous journey, which, since the advent of Christianity, scholars of Ewe history often equated to the biblical Jewish exodus from Egypt in search of the Promised Land. Ever since the Notsie episode, the Ewes are also said to have been cautious of centralized political authority, because of its autocratic tendencies. This is a factor which partly explains the failure of Ewes to come together to build large empires and kingdoms, as their Akan-speaking neighbours to the east of the River (now Lake) Volta did in pre-colonial times.

The rest of this chapter presents aspects of the Botoku histories, myths and legends, which I believe are highly relevant to understanding development, or the quest for a better future, from the point of view of my research group. The most obvious is the migration out of the walled city of Notsie in order to escape servitude. Related to this were the subsequent struggles of the new settlers to assert their autonomy against a range of external pressures: slave raiders, neighbouring powerful expansionary states, as well as German and later British colonial rule. The main point to be highlighted is that, for 300-400 years or so since Notsie, until as recently as the post independent years of the 1960s, the Botoku people had never really known one of the essential prerequisites or building blocks for development, namely, freedom. The role of *afemenunya,* or wisdom from tradition, in helping the people negotiate this difficult, and often violent journey, and the implications of the experience for the way this particular African community perceives development is also highlighted here.

According to my study participants, the desire for a better future has always been an integral part of their being. Safety from enemy attacks provided the impetus for the Notsie rulers to build a walled city; a sanctuary for the protection of their citizens, in the first instance. But because of greed, the same walled city became a prison where Agorkoli kept his subjects and put them to work until they dropped dead. Greed, they said, is like being intoxicated. Once it gets into your head, there is no turning back. To amuse himself and his stooges, Agorkoli would ask his subjects to perform stupid and impossible tasks. He asked his subjects to make rope out of clay to be used for the thatch roofing of his house. Anyone who was not able to perform the task was killed instantly, simply to put fear into others. The stupid and impossible tasks were also an excuse to sell his people into slavery. When people harvested their crops, they had to give a share of the harvest to Agorkoli. Because he was so greedy he kept asking for a greater share of the harvest from the people. The same thing applied to hunting. Any hunter returning from an expedition was required to give a large share of the game to Agorkoli and his stooges. This meant everyone was working for the enjoyment of and to support the wicked Agorkoli and his friends, and those doing the work often went hungry.

The thing on everyone's mind, certainly, was how to escape the walled city. Agorkoli's secrete police were everywhere and so no one dared to even whisper to each other about escaping. They could never trust the person they were talking to not to be an informant, so everyone just kept going as if nothing was happening. Secretly, many family groups made their own plans. One old man was kind and very wise. He told all the women who did the cooking and washing to pour the waste water on one particular spot of the wall surrounding the city. This had to be done discretely and no one was to know what they were doing. The women had no idea why they were asked to do this but because he was wise and respected, they trusted him and did as he asked. After a long time of pouring the dirty water on the wall, the old man woke everyone in the family group up in the middle of the night. They were asked to pack their few valuable belongings: digging sticks, spears, beans, fire sticks, corn flour and cooking pots. Meanwhile, the men were busy using their digging sticks to bore a hole in the wall at the exact spot the women had been flooding. The whole family group, children, old people, women and men, all escaped under cover of darkness.

They knew that at first daylight, Agorkoli's soldiers would almost certainly discover they had escaped. Agorkoli would then order the most brutal of his troops to chase after the escapees and bring them back to face his wrath. Instant execution or slavery would almost certainly be their punishment. To confuse Agorkoli's soldiers, the old man who arranged the escape, asked the group to split into four. That is, each of the four brothers and their wives and children had to go in different directions, at least for the initial stage of the journey. When Agorkoli's soldiers discovered the escapees went in four different directions, it would make it harder for them to decide which group was worth chasing. Going in different directions would also ensure that, even if Agorkoli's men caught some groups, the others could still survive to tell the tale. It is the old saying: you can't put all your palm oil in one pot. So the old man asked each group to proceed in different directions for the rest of that first night and the whole of the following day without stopping. At nightfall each group was to stop wherever they were to sleep. He said they should make sure they had enough rest during the night to regain their energy for the next day's travels. At first daylight on the following day, they were told to continue the journey in the direction of a particular mountain.

The old man said that, in the days when he was still strong and hunting, it took him only a few days and nights to get to that mountain. Whichever group got there first should set up camp and wait for the others. The place was abundant in game and so they could hunt, smoke and replenish their stock of dried meat. The women could also plant the bean seeds in case they had to wait a long time for the other groups to arrive. Not too long after the escape from Notsie, the four families reunited. Happy the whole group escaped Agorli's wrath intact, they continued the journey as one happy family. But their happiness did not last long. The difficult journey took the group in a westerly direction until they came to a place called Hodzo, near present day Ho. The people of Hodzo refused them passage through their territory and so they had to fight a bitter war in order to pass through. It was a time during which many other groups were fleeing from Agorkoli's tyranny seeking new homes. It was also a time when itinerant traders raided and captured small unsuspecting family groups for sale to coastal slave merchants. This meant most groups were suspicious of each others' intentions and those carving out territories for themselves jealously protected their boundaries.

The war at Hodzo led to the first major breakup of the escaping family group when a sub-unit of the group got lost during the confused and bitter struggle for survival. After the sad loss of one of the four family groups at Hodzo, the rest of the group continued the journey, stopping at intervals to rest and replenish their stock of smoked meat and beans; the main staples apart from wild yam, fruits and fresh game. At each replenishing camp, teams of hunters were sent in different directions to scout the lands beyond them to determine the most promising areas for permanent settlement. On one occasion, the team of hunters returned to report good news. They found a vast expanse of land full of rivers and creeks and game. The only problem was that to get there, they had to cross a big river, which we now call River Dayi. After several stops to rest and replenish their food stock, the group finally arrived at the banks of the River Dayi. Togbe Alagadawoe, the spiritual leader of the group at the time, poured libation, an offering of bean flour mixed with water, to the ancestors for safe crossing of the river. From there it took only a few days to locate the place now called Botoku; a large valley surrounded by chains of hills that formed a semi-circle from the west

32

to the eastern parts of the valley. Thus ended a most difficult and dangerous journey from Notsie. Evidence suggests this Botoku settlement occurred sometime in the late 18th century.

The escaping ancestral family group did not plan to settle at any of the replenishing camps for too long, but it takes a whole season to plant, harvest and dry bean seeds before the group could pack and continue the next phase of the journey. In the meantime, some families became reluctant to leave behind the crops and shelters they had worked hard to establish at the various camps, all to continue a difficult and risky journey to a final destination no one knew. As the group became bigger, family disputes and misunderstandings too became inevitable. For these and other reasons, on several occasions, families split up and went their own ways. As Ewe people say, when two calabashes are placed on the surface of water in a container, they will, by all means, knock at each other from time to time. That is, so long as people live in relationships to each other, there will always be conflicts and misunderstandings. So the question for them was not whether there would be conflicts or not, but rather, how families dealt with their differences. The different break away groups along the journey, including the family lost during the Hodzo war, have all reconnected with each other since the improvements in communications brought about by the availability of motor transport from the 1930s. These groups, Botoku included, now constitute six sister towns and villages within a 150 km radius of the Volta Region of Ghana. All six sister towns and villages come together from time to time to commemorate their difficult and adventurous journey. They support each other during the funerals of important chiefs. They also support major development projects in each others' villages and towns.

Since the permanent settlement, the Botoku family group evolved into the present day seven, distinct but related, clan groups of Botoku. Each clan has its own hereditary male and female chiefs. As a result of political transformations and changes over time, the last of the clan groups to form eventually came to assume the role of paramount or senior chief (*fiaga*) over the whole village. Each of the clan groups had specialized politico-military roles for the defense of the settlement, as well as for resolving conflicts between individuals or among clan groups. Despite the political changes resulting from the German colonial rule from the 1880's to the First World War, followed by British colonial rule and the United Nations mandate through to political independence as modern Ghana in 1957, the basic politico-military structure established since permanent settlement, survived relatively intact until today. Significantly, these governance structures, based on a combination of chieftaincy and clan groups, will become the main instrument for the social mobilization of Botoku citizens, both those living at home and outside, for the purposes of communal labour and financial contribution towards development projects.

An important institution the Botoku people believed assisted them in negotiating these difficult journeys was religion, initially their deities or gods and the belief systems associated with them, but increasingly the newly introduced Christian faith. The war god (Avazorli) was the most powerful of all the gods when they arrived at Botoku. He was the unifying factor for the various family groups during the migration and was believed to be responsible for maintaining confidence and hope that a permanent home, free from servitude and enemy attacks, was ahead. Other gods were soon established. All the main rivers, creeks and water holes promising abundant water supplies and food for the new settlement soon became important deities. Atsave Creek, which runs across the settlement, became an important god of peace. Kpe, Avatume, Axotoe, Dodo were all declared deities with dedicated priests who performed rituals in honour of these creeks and water holes.

Stringent taboos evolved to define the relationships between the people and their newly acquired deities and the environment. For example, no-one could remove firewood, cut down trees, or clear the adjoining lands to any of these creeks and water holes. A woman, during her menstruation, could not visit the creeks to take water or wash. Periodic offerings of corn flour mixed with palm oil, chicken, and later goats or sheep, were offered to these deities. These gods remained important for a very long time, and some are still revered to this day.

As time passed, the people continued to routinely acquire new gods and protective charms for different purposes, according to their changing circumstances. For example, sometime after the initial Botoku settlement, a hunter went on an expedition near the River Volta. He saw a very strange thing, which was to have long-term consequences for the fortunes of the new settlement: a water hole in the thick forest. Inside the water hole was a fresh water crocodile said to be carrying a small black clay pot on its head. The pot contained some herbs, which the hunter recognized and would later use for healing. The hunter promptly reported the bizarre encounter to the elders of the village. Overwhelmed with fear and reverence, they instantly declared the site a deity and the hunter the inaugural priest. The descendants of this hunter continue to provide priests for this shrine to this day. The shrine soon became popular as a place people were healed from all sorts of illnesses and misfortunes. Located close to a thriving trade route along the Volta River, the shrine also developed a reputation as a god of trade. Traders from far and near came to seek blessings for their commerce to prosper. They made promises that, if the god helped them prosper, they would pay back a set amount of cowry shells (the medium of exchange at the time), chicken, sheep or goats, depending on the status of the person making the promise.

Acquiring a new god did not at all imply giving up the previous ones. On the contrary, the new strengthened and enhanced the old. A story is told of a powerful man in more recent times, who was said to have acquired as many as 130 deities and protective charms during his lifetime. The problem was that each of the deities and charms required their own specific rituals, which he had to remember to perform. The gods became too numerous for him to recall the rituals associated with each, especially as he got older and began losing his memory. In the end, one of the protective gods ended up, quite ironically, killing him (in 1980) as punishment for failing to discharge his ritual obligations. So, whatever god people worshipped or believed protected them, it did not preclude the addition of others. On the contrary, the normal thing at the time, for any serious person, was to keep adding new and exciting protective powers to their existing stock. It was in this context that the introduction of Christianity into Botoku, at least in the formative stages, was regarded by many people; as simply another new protective deity to be added to the old stock.

The story is told that a Botoku man visiting the nearby village (Vakpo) was the first to listen to the new gospel. The gospel was introduced into Eweland by the Basel Mission (from Germany), since Germany declared a colony over the present day Volta Region of Ghana and Togo from 1885. The Botoku man was enthralled by the alleged power of Christ and the all-mighty God to conquer all evil. The biblical division of the spirit world into evil and good was familiar to Ewe people, who also believe the whole world is full of spirits, both diabolical and good. The miracles Jesus was believed to have performed while triumphing over evil were particularly appealing to the man. The man returned to Botoku with the good news and invited four of his close friends to join him to listen to the sermon the following Sunday. His friends were equally enthralled and so the five returned every Sunday to listen to the new sermon. After a while, the five men from Botoku appealed to the preacher at the nearly Vakpo church to assist them with establishing their own church at Botoku. An Akan-speaking man, Mr Otu, was posted by the Basel Mission as the first priest of the Botoku church, which opened in 1896. This was soon followed by an infant school in 1899. Both the new church and the school soon collapsed, partly because Mr. Otu conducted the sermons and lessons in Akan, which although believed to be spoken widely at Botoku at the time, was still a second language.

An Ewe-speaking teacher-priest was posted in 1906 and with that, both the church and the school revived, and rapidly developed into important institutions that would have serious consequences for community development in later years. The chiefs and elders assigned a dedicated plot of land to the new converts to build their mission (at present day Kpodzi) and where they could practice their new faith unhindered from traditional ritual and taboo obligations. Unlike the additive nature of Ewe gods and deities, it soon became clear the new faith required its followers to give up their pre-existing gods and other cultural practices. For some new converts, it all became too hard and they gave up and reverted to their traditional practices.

In 1918, when four Botoku students from a nearby boarding school for teachers and priests who were back on holidays suddenly died one after the other, apparently as a result of the world-wide influenza of that year which killed an estimated 100,000 in the British Gold Coast Colony alone (Patterson, 1981), the incident was attributed to illicit affairs they had with widows in the village. Traditionally women who lost their husbands must abstain from sexual intercourse for a period of two planting seasons (one year) while men abstained for one season. The new converts however were free from these customs and traditions. The incident shocked both believers and non-believers alike. The event brought home to the people that Christianity might not be as capable of providing security as some first thought. The choice for many converts was either to abandon the new faith altogether, or to accept it outwardly while protection was secretly sought under traditional cults. Since then Botoku people, like people in many parts of Africa, have found creative if bizarre ways of accommodating and adapting new faiths to suit their needs.

Today, about 90 per cent of Botoku people will identify as Christians. The original German Presbyterian church, and the later Catholic faith, remains the two orthodox churches. In addition to these are a variety of permutations of Africanist churches combining elements of indigenous practices with the Bible. My last count in 2002 identified 11 such churches. While the new faith and education conflicted with traditional Ewe spiritual and religious practices, the new institutions, in other ways, rather reinforced traditional Ewe patriarchy and gendered divisions of labour. For example, out of the new church-school were to emerge, by the 1st World War, the veteran Botoku scholars including David Dankwa, Michael Asemda and Sam Darko, men who graduated from Amedsofe Seminary to become teachers. Their female counterparts were Christiana Afaribea, Charllote Ampoti and Selina Noagbesenu, who acquired further training in cookery and dressmaking at the Ho Women Training Institute. This patriarchal Christian educational tradition would have long-term implications for issues of gender equity in present day development discourses.

For the Botoku people, the greatest threat to their quest for a better future since permanent settlement was the constant fear of slave raiders, and the territorial ambitions of the neighbouring Akan expansionary states wanting to subjugate smaller vulnerable groups. I will draw upon three stories to elaborate the point made earlier that, until as recently as the post colonial era from the 60s, the Botoku people had never really experienced the most fundamental prerequisite for development. The first of these stories states that, soon after arriving at Botoku the new settlers discovered a thriving trade route along the River Volta, involving coastal traders who brought dried fish, salt and European goods for sale. In return, the traders bought palm oil, wild yams, ivory and slaves, to take back to the coast. Located in close proximity to the banks of the Volta, Botoku people took advantage of this thriving trade by producing and selling palm oil, dried cassava and yams to trade for salt and European goods. The Botoku claimed a group of Akan-speaking traders residing along the river were raiding Botoku traders for their goods and capturing the traders, who were then taken back to Akanland across the Volta to become domestic slaves, or sold to itinerant coastal slave merchants. There was a feeling of defeat that, after all that time escaping from Agorkoli, they were again faced with threats of enemy attacks and enslavement. In response, powerful hunters were dispatched to spy on the small Akan settlement so they could determine their numerical strength. Once convinced Botoku had the advantage in numbers, the *asafowo* (youth and warriors) marched under the cover of darkness and captured the Akan traders believed to be raiding the Botoku traders. They brought them to Botoku and shared them among the three leading clan groups. One clan integrated their captives into the body politic through marriage over time. The second, the clan who ruled over the whole village at the time, integrated some through marriage but also sacrificed some to their

37

gods. The third clan group did not integrate their captives but instead, gave them land to function as a separate clan group of their own, although over time they too inter-married into the broader Botoku society. The men were said to be very dark, tall and handsome, and hence succeeded in marrying into some of the most powerful Botoku families of the day. These captives, and their descendants, were believed to have introduced the present day Akan art of chieftaincy to Botoku. They have remained the paramount rulers of Botoku to this day. This story, according to my sources, is significant not only because it shows how pervasive slavery was at the time but also because it highlights the fact there is a hardly a 'pure' Botoku family and that outsiders are absorbed and integrated into the body politic throughout the society, right from the paramount ruling families through to the other clan groups. This is why, in the broader view, Botoku has always been a welcome place for new ideas and people.

The other story relates to how human sacrifice became taboo in Botoku. Sometime after the settlement, a Botoku hunter was said to have fallen seriously ill after return from a hunting expedition. The man was brought to the shrine of the thriving god of trade and fortune. This was the new deity of trade, located close to the Volta River trade route, which was by then attracting visitors from all over the region for the purposes of healing, as well as offering pledges to the god for good fortune. Before healing could take place, the priest had to be possessed by the deity, which would then instruct the priest on what treatment to provide. In this case, the possessed priest declared the man was sick because he had contaminated the deity of trade and fortune with human blood. Apparently the man had returned to the village from his hunting expedition with a human skull as sacrifice to one of his clan deities. The priest instructed the man to return the human skull to wherever it came from. The priest declared that human blood was a serious taboo to the new and popular god of trade and good fortune. From that time it was taboo for any Botoku person, whether living at home or outside, to participate in, or witness human sacrifice. According to my informants, the reason behind the deity's decision to declare human sacrifice taboo was apparently to prevent the development of Agorkoli's brutal and autocratic type of chieftaincy in the new settlement. It was also to protect the deity's flourishing reputation as god of trade and fortune, which was bringing material wealth to the priests in charge. For this reputation to continue, visitors and traders needed to feel safe to travel, free of harassment. This latter story, apart from confirming the widespread nature of itinerant raids on unsuspecting victims for ritual or enslavement purposes, also challenges the widely held view within the present day development fraternity, that African customs and traditions do not change, and hence constitute insurmountable barriers to economic development or wealth creation. What this latter story shows is that, where economic interests are at stake, the custodians of the spiritual and religious norms and practices, even those people often believe are hardest to change, are prepared to act and adapt in order to protect their material interests.

The third, and final story, is how Botoku came to be known by its current name. The story was repeated many times throughout the research that originally, the people were called Dzali, after their powerful god (Awadzali) reputed to have guided them from Notsie to the present settlement. This original name remained in use until as recently as late 19th century when it changed to Botoku. It all started when, after a period of rumour, uncertainty and fear of impending invasions, a contingent of Ashanti fighters from the present day Ashanti Region of Ghana did arrive at the Volta River basin (1869). In order to understand the significance of this event it is important to go back decades, if not centuries, to the time of the permanent settlement, to explain the perennial attempts by the more powerful Akan-speaking neighbours to extend their political hegemony over the smaller autonomous Ewe clan and family groups recently arrived from Notsie. As far as Dzali were concerned, the most significant of the expansionary states was the Akwamu, which demanded tributary payments in people and money from smaller entities such as Dzali. Although they had never really accepted such tributary obligations, on occasion Dzali had no choice but to pay in order to keep the peace. It was in the context of this refusal to pay tributaries by many of the tiny autonomous Ewe villages, that Akwamu invited the most powerful of all the expansionary states at the time, Ashanti (claimed to have occupied an area larger than the present day Ghana at the peak of its power), to help the former asset its authority. Dzali's location, in close proximity to the Volta River which the Ashanti had to across in order to access the Ewe communities, made it particularly vulnerable. When the Ashanti fighters arrived at the bank of the Volta they were unable to cross the river because they had no canoes. Besides, most of them had never seen such a large and rapidly flowing river and were frightened of it. Given the reputation of Ashanti fighters, the Dzali people decided it would be suicidal to take them on directly. Instead, they offered to ferry the Ashanti fighters in canoes, a few people at a time, across the river.

Knowing their Ashanti passengers could not swim, as soon as the canoes were out of sight and in the deepest parts of the river, the Dzali farers deliberately capsized the boats, thus drowning the Ashanti fighters in small numbers. This apparently went on for a long time until the secret was finally uncovered. In exasperation, the invaders described the Dzali as 'obutu kurofuo,' meaning 'those who capsize boats.' With time, this Akan expression was corrupted to Botoku, which eventually replaced Dzali. (This probably explains why early German maps of the area in the 1880s named the village variously as Dzali or the hyphenated Botoku-Dzali).

Meanwhile, in order to repel the invading forces, several tiny autonomous Ewe entities formed temporary alliances among themselves. The trouble for the Botoku people was that they did not have gun powder for their guns (which had long since replaced bows and arrows as the main instrument of war throughout West Africa) in order to join the alliance. In desperation, the person charged with the responsibility for leading the Botoku troops offered his own sister as *awuba* (pawn) to a gun powder seller in a nearby village in return for gun powder. He was also said to have sold three men from his family as slaves. All these, according to my informants, indicated the extent of the sacrifice that had to be made in the face of the looming threats.

The rest of the story then became a long catalogue of human suffering and devastation brought about by months of raids and counter raids during which bands of retreating Ashanti fighters succeeded in taking Botoku men, women, children and sacred objects as booties back home. While some of the captives did return, others ended up as domestic slaves or were sold for exports. Clearly, the general volatility of the pre-colonial feudal socio-economic environment constituted real constraints to meaningful development.

The internecine wars and raids in the region declined under colonial rule following the 1885 Berlin Conference where, with the aid of a large wall map of Africa, the major European powers literally carved out the continent among themselves, creating the most artificial and disruptive territorial boundaries ever known in history. Not surprisingly, as the threats from slave raids and wars abated, they were quickly replaced by new pressures and disruptions associated with externally imposed authoritarian regimes. The significance of these stories, from the point of view of development, is that until as recently as the last 50 years, most Ghanaian and Western African societies lacked the basic freedom to go about their day to day business in

40

peace and without fear. Thus, during the formative stages of German colonial rule, at the turn of the 20th century for example, the Botoku paramount chief was said to have had a cordial relationship with the visiting officials and was even commended by them for granting a plot of land to the new Basel Mission church to cultivate a cocoa farm. His successor though remained only a regent or acting chief from the point of view of the German District Commissioner (DC), who refused to recognize him as chief because of the latter's perpetual refusal to obey colonial orders, especially with regards to forced labour. This, he and his elders, and indeed all the able-bodied men did, by frequently escaping from the village at the sight of visiting officials to take sanctuary in the thick forests of the Volta basin.

Another Botoku paramount chief, this time under British rule following the departure of the Germans after defeat in the First World War, was said to be plagued by frequent threats and attempts to remove him from office by his own people, until he had no choice but to abdicate the stool. Part of his problem was the difficulty in balancing the customary expectations of being a chief versus accommodating the interests and pressures of the nascent Christian community. Another part of his problem was the difficulty in compelling his people to provide forced labour and pay *lampo* (tax) that the British needed in order to build their colonial infrastructure. This task was rendered all the more difficult for many chiefs at the time because of the Gold Coast Aboriginal Rights Protection Society's popular and effective slogan during most of the colonial period of no taxation without representation.

How best to protect the physical environment was also a constant source of conflict between the Botoku people and the macro administrative authorities that assumed control over the region over time, both colonial and post independent. The problem, my informants emphasized, was not so much that the people were against efforts to protect and maintain the ecological environment. Rather, it was the way successive governments have gone about it. Indeed, the greatest mistakes of governments of all persuasion to this day, appear to be the tendency to ignore or at best pay only lip service to local knowledge. The assumption is that governments, with the aid of technical knowledge, know what is best for local people.

A focus group *tsiami* or spokesperson, a teacher by profession, explained. One of the first things the Germans did on arrival (apart from demand for forced labour) was to pass forestry laws (in 1890s) designed to protect the environment. Under the law, it became an offence for anybody to remove timber, hunt, clear land along rivers and creeks or hilltops for farming and other purposes within designated forest reserves. For some, the laws were simply designed to deprive them of their livelihoods and so made no sense to them. For others, it was a matter of autonomy and the right to decide how best to protect their own forests and water sources. After all, although they may not have referred to it in environmental terms, commitment to ensuring an appropriate balance between people and their ecological environment was an important part of the ancient wisdom that their ancestors brought with them from the Notsie walled-city. This is why one of the first decisions the new settlers made was to declare all the rivers, water holes, hill tops and caves deities or gods. Stringent customs and taboos were in place to regulate the relationships between the people and their environments. As noted (Chapter 4), people could not clear land or remove wood within certain proximity of these deities, visits occurred on certain days of the week only, women in their menstrual periods could not visit or wash themselves in certain rivers and water holes, etc. That is why traditionally a person planning to fell ten palm trees in order to produce palm wine, for example, was expected to plant twenty palm seedlings (twice the number of mature trees) during the rainy season prior to the season when the trees were actually felled. Instant punishment such as snake bites, accidents and unexplained illnesses and other misfortunes ensured that the people respected these customs and taboos. Such sanctions also meant that people generally did not take more than what they needed to sustain themselves from the land.

But all that changed with the arrival of Christianity. The biggest mistake the missionaries made according to the *tsiami* or spokesperson was to promote the arrogant blanket view that all the local traditions and customs were 'pagan' and hence unchristian. So the new converts were the first to start violating these ancient traditions such as indiscriminate removal of wood and clearing sacred lands. It was therefore adding insult to injury in the tsiami or spokesperson's view when the same Germans and later British who supported the Christians to undermine traditional authority suddenly turned round saying to the chiefs and elders we now want to teach you how to take care of your environment. This is why, despite efforts by governments to maintain forest reserves in the area, the local Botoku people have at best treated these reserves with indifference and on occasion actively sabotaged such initiatives. Stories were told about how forestry workers sent to demarcate the mandated government reserves were often chased away by cutlass wielding local people.

Also, cited was a more recent government forestry scheme to illustrate the importance of valuing local knowledge. Following the inundation of hunting and farming grounds by the Volta hydroelectric dam (in the 1960s) and the consequent pressures on arable lands, the newly independent Ghana government decided to return portions of the forest reserves to the local people for cultivation. Under the scheme, local people would clear the land and plant their crops. Government forestry workers would have free access to the farms to plant tieak seedlings for timber, the farmers being expected to water the seedlings and take care of them. Profits from the timber were to be shared between government and the farmers. But the farmers were more interested in continuing access to land for growing their crops rather than profits from timber plantations. What did the farmers do? Without making a big fuss, each time they boiled food on their farms to eat, the farmers simply poured the hot water around the base of the young and tender teak seedlings. The result was that only few of the seedlings survived to become timber trees. The point about all these stories the *tsiami* or spokesperson concluded was the need for governments and policy makers to understand that the key to bringing about change is to respect and value local knowledge.

To conclude this chapter, the important question posed by my sources (previous chapter) was not so much why, how and when these historical events, sometimes difficult and dehumanizing as they may be happened, but rather, what the meanings associated with the events can teach people today about Botoku and its people. What this means is that if we really want to understand development and how to achieve it in this particular context, we need to start with the values, attitudes and orientations to life that helped, or did not help, along peoples' difficult and challenging journeys. Key to this process is capacity to routinely work out the things that we really need to be safe and happy as humans versus the things that, no matter how much we desire or want them, may add very little to our ability to be happy. For them, the quest for a better future means people must be prepared to draw a line in the sand over how much tyranny and hardship they are willing to endure in any situation. The problem is not so much whether there are difficulties or not, but how one chooses to understand or interpret and deal with them. It means having hope, no matter how difficult the circumstances. Without hope people cannot summon the strength to change anything.

These narratives remind us about the inevitability of change and the great capacity of people to adapt to change. Critically important is willingness to accept, and where possible, influence the processes of change rather than expending often precious resources fighting things that sooner or later are bound to change anyway. It also means preparedness to take risks, though it is important that people are clever about the risks they take. Patience is important to be able to work out the most strategic point at which to act. It also requires sacrifice for the benefit of the whole group. Although unity is important, people must also be prepared to accept that, even within the same family, not everyone's destiny will be the same. Sometimes it is necessary for each family group to go their different ways in the hopes that, if some perish, others may survive to tell the tale. As one informant reflected regarding the alleged drowning of the invading Ashanti fighters, *eno dziwo meseo nadze deka,* literally 'when your mother borne you and you are not strong you have to be handsome or beautiful.' What this means is that every person, no matter their circumstances, is endowed with some special gift or strength and that life is all about the capacity to routinely evaluate one's strengths and limitations and appropriately draw upon strengths in meeting challenges as they arise.

A major lesson from these, especially for those in decision-making positions is that, as ruler, you cannot rule over an empty land. As a ruler you can only rule over people, but the people must be willing to be ruled over. Today, if a chief or a person in authority repeatedly misuses their power, that person is asked to remember what happened to Agorkoli and his greedy friends. They are also reminded of the extent to which people were prepared to vote with their feet, so to speak, in order to escape the colonial demands for forced labour and *lampo* (taxes), all for the quest for freedom and autonomy. These, and similar stories, often make the person rethink.

Stories like this are relevant today as reminders to politicians and civil servants across Africa of the dangers of taking the people over whom they exercise authority for granted. These values, beliefs and general orientations to life permeating my informants' narratives, is what Botoku, and indeed other Ewe-speaking people call *afemenunya* (knowldge that comes from the home), akin to the Aristotlean concept of practical wisdom or situational ethics (Flyvbjerg, 2001; Schram & Caterino, 2006; Tsey, 2010). Like the ancient Greeks, Ewe people of Ghana distinguish between several categories of knowledge (Dzobo, 1992), believing possession of *afemenunya* (wisdom) is the key to building healthy relationships and communities. A person possessing *afemenunya* knows how to appropriately conduct himself, or herself, in any given circumstance, and displays qualities such as respect, patience, dignity, freedom, autonomy, sacrifice, fairness, forgiveness, obedience and humility. These, and related qualities, are traditionally considered and sought after when selecting leaders and chieftains.

These qualities, my study participants repeated, contrasted with *sukuu nunya* (school knowledge), which they fear is the only type of knowledge young people of today have the opportunity to learn because of the social changes to which I already referred. Knowledge from formal education, they felt, was associated with such qualities as precision, being on time and immutability. While they regarded both types of knowledge as being highly relevant in modern society, they were concerned modernization and social change meant more people were acquiring *sukununya,* but not necessarily *afemenunya.* To illustrate the point, they cite how educational qualifications, technocratic skills and expertise, but not necessarily wisdom, have become the main criteria for appointment into positions of authority in contemporary Ghana. This relative marginalization of wisdom has been widely documented by social and political scientists. The complex development challenges of the 21st require more than ever before ethical and moral approaches for working out what is right and wrong as a necessary, if not the leading, part of the solutions. For Ghana and other African countries, the relative marginalization of wisdom may well explain some of the governance, and other social challenges, such as corruption, selfishness and greed, currently confronting them. Oral histories such as this may constitute opportunities to restore *afemenunya* (wisdom) to its legitimate place in contemporary societies, not only in Africa, but probably the world at large. The rest of this book, in many ways, describes the Botoku people's attempts to apply wisdom, with varying degrees of success, in negotiating and mediating their efforts towards a quest for a better future through such mechanisms as community infrastructure building, cultural reform, economic participation and connections to ancestral homelands.

Asafo or warriors enacting the past

Chapter 5

From Road Building in the 1930s to Middle School in the 50's

This chapter describes the origin, planning, and the process of implementing two of the early community infrastructure projects; some of my main interests in embarking on the oral history project in the first place. The two projects I will focus on are a dirt road built in the 1930s, which enabled motor cars to access the village for the first time, and a non-Christian secular four-year middle school, built in the 1950s. These two projects have one thing in common: they are both good examples of community initiated projects undertaken in the context of European colonial rule in Africa. The road was installed during the hey-day of the British West African Empire in the 1930s, and the middle school at a time when the empire was rapidly fading away after WWII.

Through the two case studies, I will attempt to clarify three main points. First, I will describe a long and vibrant community development, or self-help tradition; a tradition which, significantly, had its origins in the ancient migration and settlement politico-military structures described previously. The second point I will illustrate is the importance of local development elites in initiating development projects and the changes in the composition of these development elites over time. Of particular interest here is the increased role non-resident citizens played as the main originators of development projects from the 1950s, due in part to the rapid rural-urban migration for education and employment opportunities. The third, and final point I will discuss in the chapter is that, even for the smallest self-initiated grass roots micro-community development projects, such as those described here, the overall macro-government policy environment can be critical in determining the extent to which such projects succeeded or not. While some macro-policy environments are enabling of micro-community interests and aspirations, others are explicitly or implicitly disabling of them, even though both governments and communities may sometimes profess to be aspiring to achieve the same goals. Colonial governments, by the very nature of being imposed from the outside, often act with little regard for the aspirations of the local populations. This results in severe disconnect between the

47

objectives of the rulers, no matter how well meaning, and the needs and interest of the ruled. Not surprisingly, my informants were quick to liken some of the excesses of successive colonial regimes, and indeed aspects of the subsequent newly independent Ghanaian draconian laws, to Agorkorli's brutal and autocratic regime.

One of the earliest self-help projects critically important for the social, economic and spiritual development of Botoku in the 20th century, was a 13km dirt road that would eventually allow the first motor vehicle to enter Botoku (about 1937). Built in the 1930s, this path initially connected Botoku to nearby Vakpo and was later extended, in the opposite direction, for another 5 km to nearby Tsoxor, for a total of 18 km. This dirt road was by no means the first 'road' to be constructed. It was however the first, my sources emphasized, that they decided on their own accord to build, and it was the first motor vehicle friendly one. Before the construction of the dirt road there were roads in the area built by the Germans when they had a barrack (customs service) at Botoku. This was located on the German side only half a kilometre from the colonial border with the British and existed until the First World War. These roads were narrow, hilly and had many curves. The early roads were clearly not built for cars but as a mode to carry the DC (District Commissioner) in hammock as they toured their newly acquired territories.

Some of the pioneer Botoku cocoa farmers at the time were worried about transporting their cocoa and other farm produce to the nearest market (Vakpo) for sale. These farmers had seen motor trucks in Vakpo transporting cocoa and other goods. They were convinced a road for motor trucks would not only benefit their cocoa farms, it would also allow Botoku people to sell food crops, chewing stick, sponge, palm oil and other produce at the market centers more frequently than the existing practice of head loading (carrying produce on the head) allowed. The new cocoa farms were located 5-15km from the Botoku village itself. The challenge facing the new growers was how to head load the crop the distance from the farms to the village, and then at least another 14km from the village to Vakpo. Accordingly, the pioneer cocoa farmers approached Togbe Tamtia IV (paramount chief) and his elders about the idea of building a road from Botoku to Vakpo for motor vehicles to carry their cocoa and other trade goods to the nearest markets. Togbe did not hesitate in assembling his people to discuss the plan. The idea was initially opposed by some who said they didn't have cocoa farms and so did not see how the road would benefit them. Others feared their economic trees, like coffee, cocoa, kola, palm trees and odum (timber) would be destroyed as a result of the proposed road passing through their lands.

By far the main obstacle to the proposed road was convincing an increasingly cynical population, whose previous experience with 'road' building and maintenance and the associated head loading of colonial officials and their belongings, had left a bad feeling among many people. Constructing and looking after *afomoe* (footpaths) to their farming, hunting and sacred lands, to the creeks and water holes for collecting water, to their favourite market centers, as well as establishing links with families in nearby villages and farm settlements had always been part of their existence; but so too was head loading of things along these pathways.

Botoku people, it was explained to me, were always on the lookout for ways to make life more bearable for themselves and their children, and would take advantage of any opportunity, so long as it suited their situation. Opportunities, they believed, did not come to people. This is why, as a people, they had always valued travelling, for it is through travel that people stumble across new ideas. As the Ewes say, it is the child who has never travelled outside their village who thinks their mother's soup is the best. This means, unless people travel beyond their immediate environments, they never get exposed to new ideas and opportunities.

The opportunity to exchange and sell their excess produce for the things they did not have or could not produce themselves, such as salt, had always been part of their quest for travel. This was long before their departure from Notsie in search of a permanent settlement. Since settlement, the Botoku people had taken part in a wide variety of trading activities, especially along the Volta River trade routes, exchanging such items as chewing stick for cleaning teeth, sponge for washing the body, smoked meat, palm oil and other food crops, in return for which they obtained their salt supplies, matches and other European goods from coastal traders. Stories were told about itinerant Botoku traders and travellers going on long trips across the Volta into Akanland that took months, and years, and in some cases the traders never returned at all. The latter were presumed to have settled on their own accord or enslaved and absorbed into other villages. The reason these stories were important was in highlighting the fact that, so long as the Botoku people were left to use the new ideas being introduced, first by the Germans and later the British, in ways they saw fit, they were happy to embrace new ideas and opportunities. This included introductions such as the Christian faith, education, trade skills in carpentry and bricklaying, cash cropping, and so on. Many people initially opposed the road, because it reminded them of their experience with forced labour under the Germans and later the British.

The story was told of how the DC did their visits in hammock. When the DC arrived at Tsrukpe (a nearby village) the chiefs there would provide ten to 15 able-bodied men to carry him in hammock as well as head load his belongings and those of his entourage to Botoku. Botoku chiefs would provide people to carry him to Wusuta (another nearby village) and so on. Mango trees, some of which can be seen today, were planted alongside the early German roads in order to provide shade for the DC and his entourage. If the DC arrived in a village and there was no recognized chief available or willing to commandeer his people to relieve the porters, then those porters had no choice but to continue the journey to other villages until sufficient groups of new porters were recruited to replace them. Sometimes this could make it weeks and months before porters were able to make it back to their own villages. Because the forced labour was unpopular, not many Botoku chiefs were willing to compel the people to participate for fear of losing public support. This was particularly true at a time when the growing Christian community flouted the authority of the chiefs and elders by breaking age old taboos, such as not removing wood or clearing land adjoining the sacred creeks, water holes and hill sides. The chiefs, fearing more serious breaks with custom, were careful not to antagonize the broader population too much. To illustrate their point, the story was told of a Botoku paramount chief who escaped the German colonial authority, by going into self-imposed 'exile' for many years, taking sanctuary in the thick forest near the Volta.

Another reason for opposing the road was a fear that it would unnecessarily expose them to the growing demands of the British colonial authorities, which, since the First World War, had assumed control over the area under United Nations mandate, for communal labour and taxation. These demands, like those of the Germans before them, were likened to some of Agokoli's stupid and unbearable demands. Despite these concerns, opposition to the road did not last for too long. Those in favour of the idea were able to explain the road was not for the benefit of those growing cocoa alone, and that the whole of Botoku would benefit. The proponents of the new road, my informants consistently emphasized, were people of integrity and honour, and hence, in the long run, the people's respect and trust in them prevailed. These pioneer cocoa growers were described frequently as 'strong,' 'hard working,' 'forward looking,' and 'trustworthy' people.

The road construction, which they stressed had no government involvement, began about 1935. People contributed cash crops such as cocoa and coffee, timber, as well as money for the purchase of tools and materials. Pick axes, shades, saws, hoes and pans were among the tools and materials bought. The work was done through the efforts of communal labour. The whole town was divided into five main clan groups, each group under the direction of an energetic *asafoatse* (war leader). The groups took turns working on different days so there were people working on the road every day of the week, except on Sundays. On this day the Christians attended church and others observed *asamigbe,* or the traditional sacred day when people did not work and the priests attended to their shrines. All the bridges between Botoku and Vakpo were built by German-trained pioneer Botoku bricklayers and carpenters. Many of these, leading and respected builders of the time, were working outside Botoku as far away as Koforidua and Nkawkaw (present day Eastern region of Ghana), but were happy to take time away from their jobs in order to help with the road building. The road took about two and a half years and was completed in 1937. My research participants still fondly recalled the sense of pride, accomplishment, awe and celebration that occurred when, for the first time, people laid eyes on a motor vehicle.

Tsrukpe (a nearby village) lies between Botoku and Vakpo, yet the people there failed to take part in the construction of the road. Their reason was that they had no cocoa to sell at Vakpo and hence had nothing to gain from the road. Though Tsrukpe refused to take part in building the road, the Botoku people were still happy that at least the people there were willing to allow the road to pass through their lands and the village itself without any objection, and for that they were grateful.

Cocoa production on a significant scale at Botoku, the main motivation for building the road in the first place, never really eventuated. Despite the road proponents being referred to as pioneer and leading cocoa growers, their holdings were very small by any standards; no more than five to ten acres at the most per grower. None of these people saw cocoa farming as a full time occupation, but rather as a source of monetary income to supplement subsistence farming in an increasingly monetary economy. Also, the sub-tropical soil, once cleared of its virgin forests, quickly succumbed to intense erosion. The result was that the soil lost its nutrients and the cocoa trees withered and died after five to ten years. Besides the fragile soil, Botoku

51

did not really have tracts of land large enough to produce cocoa on bigger scales. Disappointed, some of the more committed citizens migrated to other parts of the country more suited for cocoa growing and started new farms as migrant share-croppers.

The construction of the road did not mean motor vehicle transport became readily available for Botoku people. From the time the road opened in the late 1930s, to as recently as the turn of the century, the practice had been for one or two passenger lorries, privately owned and often owner-operated, to depart the village very early each morning to take travelers to the nearby district markets and service centers. These would then return to the village with their passengers and luggage in the late afternoon. During the times in between these routinely available services, anyone needing transport into or out of the village had to walk the 18km dirt road, unless they were lucky enough to secure a lift from the rare visiting car. Although the government has taken responsibility for maintaining the road in the last ten years, it still remains unsealed and very rough. The point to understand is that, by any standards, there is nothing very striking about this road at all; it is just a simple, rugged dirt road. But, for the Botoku people, it was the first major modern infrastructure project they undertook and maintained themselves for more than 70 years. The fact that they did it all on their own accord, without pressure from the colonial authorities, made it all the more special for them. What the experience taught them, my research participants believed, was the fact that with determination, anything was possible.

This sense of achievement felt by the Botoku people is even more fully appreciated when understood within developments in the broader colonial policy contexts of the time. Unlike most parts of the world, where the invention or adoption of the wheel and vehicles drawn by horses and other beasts of burden revolutionized pre-industrial transport, Africa did not follow the trend. This failure to adapt maintained head loading as the main form of transport which, despite the recent widespread adoption of a variety of more modern alternatives, remains significant to this day. The inability of Africa to invent the wheel, according to commentators, simply confirmed their relatively low levels of intelligence and the associated technological backwardness compared with other racial groups. They argued this constituted one of the main barriers to development in Africa. To overcome this barrier, the British and other colonial powers, at least during the formative stages of their rules, tried in vain to introduce horses and other beasts of burden, for transport as well as to till the soil. Unfortunately, at least in West Africa, the animals consistently succumbed to the ravages of the sleeping sickness carried by the tsetse fly. Unable to sustain horse drawn carts and other beasts of burden in the face of this menace, the European colonial authorities resigned themselves to the traditional head loading, at least initially, as their main form of transport. Official reports on the British Gold Coast (present day Ghana) for example, described the plight of the African porter in the 'colonial transport service' at the time (Government of the Gold Coast, 1908; Tsey & Short, 1995). It stated that, with constant walking for a twelve- month period and averaging 400 miles a month (the work that year was rather harder than usual), a large number of the porters were being incapacitated by sore feet, made worse by the gravelling and metaling of some of the main roads. Among one gang of porters, the majority had their soles completely worn through. Incredibly, the solution to the sore feet, according to the reports, was to coat the porters' feet with coal tar. Coal-tar, it was said, would fill the cracks and was a good antiseptic. It also afforded some protection if applied thickly (Government of the Gold Coast, 1908). As a later commentator comically put it, the introduction of boots quickly consigned this experiment to the locker of discarded colonial remedies, and so forestalled the rise of a new breed of heavy-footed porters in Africa (Hopkins, 1973).

The reports also described how motor transportation initially developed quite slowly. The first motor vehicle to arrive on the Gold Coast was a paraffin-fired car, obtained in 1902 for use by the governor in Accra. However, this was said to be a white elephant, languishing unused in the government secretariat until, during a clean-up campaign in 1908, it was carried out and thrown into the sea. By 1908, a few lorries had been imported into the country but it was not until the years of the First World War that motor transport developed on a significant scale. This was partly because of high railway tariffs and poor maintenance of the railway stock. For most of the colonial period, until WWII, any progress made in road building was reportedly due mainly to the efforts of chiefs and their people, especially in the cocoa producing areas. According to historians, Tetteh Quarshie from Lartey, in the present day Eastern region of Ghana, introduced cocoa into Ghana in the 1880s when he smuggled the beans home from the Atlantic Portuguese colony of Fernando Po, where he worked as migrant labourer on plantations.

From there the cocoa crop spread slowly but then picked up speed in the 1910s, aided by the Basel mission, to other parts of present day southern

Ghana (Hill, 1963). The mission saw the new crop as a way of promoting the financial independence of local churches and their schools, which were expected to be financially self-sufficient. According to colonial reports, the roads were built in an *ad hoc* fashion by chiefs and cocoa farmers, as and when they felt they were necessary. As such the system that developed did not follow the guidelines of the government's policy, which stressed roads were meant to complement the railways (which it considered to be the principle arteries of communication), rather than to compete with them. The dilemma for the colonial government at the time was whether motor transport, which to a larger extent was controlled by Africans, should be allowed to compete with, and possibly run down, a colonial government railway system financed by loans borrowed from the London money market. In characteristic colonial fashion, the authorities elected to protect their own revenue needs, as well as those of metropolitan investors in the railways, by using taxation and other direct actions in their efforts to curb motor transport competition. Among the direct actions was the infamous 'road gap' policy under which gaps were deliberately maintained in portions of the road systems that were seen to be competing with the railways, so as to prevent lorries running on them. The policy was both unpopular and grossly ineffective in curbing the incidence of motor competition.

The bizarre and farcical nature of the road gap policy was not lost on a general manager of the railways who reported how alcoholic gin was transported along one of the roads affected by the policy. According to him gin for Kumasi was being lorried up the Prahsu road to Brofoyedru, head loaded to Famena over the three mile road gap, lorried from Fomena to Akrokeri, railed from Akrokeri to Bekwai, and then lorried to Kumasi. The manager, concluding the whole situation was farcical, but real, pleaded with the governor in Accra and the colonial office in London, for the road gap policy to be abolished (Tsey & Short, 1995). Botoku was far from the immediate vicinity of the railways and hence was not directly affected by the road gap policy. Besides, by the time the Botoku people built their dirt road, the gap policy had long been abolished. Nevertheless, this and other policies of the time clearly show that, whatever local communities such as Botoku achieved in terms of road building, was achieved despite an unfavourable colonial transport policy environment unduly favouring British investments in railways over and above the emerging local indigenous motor transport industry.

Similar to the road building in the 1930's, the establishment of a middle school in the 1950s was originated by groups of Botoku development elites. Unlike the originators of the road proposal though, who were all local residents with direct economic interests in the emerging cash-cropping industry, the originators of the school were non-resident Botoku citizens, all teachers working outside the village. Since the opening of a three-year infant school at Botoku at the turn of the 19th century, education was enthusiastically embraced. As noted in chapter four, by the time the British and French took Eweland from the Germans at the end of WWI and split the area among themselves under the UN mandate, Botoku had already produced groups of pioneer Christian-educated men and women, many of whom were said to fluently read and write Ewe, German, Akan, and later English. Although the original three-year infant school had developed into a six-year primary school operating at full capacity by the 1930s, there were no opportunities for the students to proceed beyond the primary level.

The story is told of how pupils at the time, who completed primary six in Botoku, had to go to neighbouring towns like Vakpo Wusuta, Have or Anfoega to continue their four-year middle school education. Understandably, this was a logistically difficult undertaking in those days. Most of the students could not go to those towns and villages, either due to financial problems, or because they could not find people with whom to lodge. Native Botoku teachers, who were all teaching outside Botoku itself at the time, met during one of the school holidays to discuss what to do so the town could move forward in education. The teachers came up with the idea of opening a middle school in the village. They met with Togbe Tamtia V and his elders to discuss the project. Togbe Tamtia V was an educated man himself, who in 1951 had become the new paramount chief. The idea was hailed by both Togbe and the elders.

Although the original idea for a school came from the emerging non-resident educated elite, the actual planning and implementation was made possible by highly committed and dedicated resident advocates for education. The notion of a middle school itself was a popular one, both at home and outside, crossing lines of people's educational background. For Botoku people living outside the village, a middle school would provide opportunities for them to send their children back home to live with family to obtain some of their schooling. Many believed this was important for connecting young people to their ancestral roots. As with the earlier road building, my research participants were keen to explain there was no government involvement in the school when it first started, and that they did it all by themselves. By the time the idea of a middle school was first broached in the 1950s, the Botoku church community had had some 50 years of experience in running their own mission primary school, with some support from the church headquarters. A secular non-church middle school, to be owned, not by the church but by the community at large, was something very rare.

The first step in making the school a reality was to obtain permission from the Ministry of Education to open a school. Next, a board of four directors was appointed to oversee the school development. The main priority for the board was to mobilize financial resources to employ a teacher for the school. All residents were asked to make contributions according to their capacity to pay. At the same time, comprehensive lists of all Botoku citizens living outside the village were compiled. Armed with these lists, two people were sent across the country to collect 'levies' from the Botoku people on the lists. After a year's preparatory work, the school duly opened with a first intake of eleven students (eight boys and three girls) in 1957, the same year Ghana became the first African country south of the Sahara to obtain independence from colonial rule.

As with the road construction in the 1930s, the story of the middle school is, in many ways, a tale of resourcefulness, determination to succeed, and the generosity of individuals. During the first year the school was in existence, the living room of one of the pioneer teacher-priests served as a classroom. The local Presbyterian church became additional space for combined classes from the second year onwards. By the third year it became clear a dedicated school building was urgently needed. An elderly lady, (the custodian of land belonging to her clan) donated a large plot for the construction of the new building. While residents provided communal labour, non-residents continued to make financial contributions towards the teachers' salaries, as well as construction of the building.

In 1961, four years after the school was originally started, a four classroom building with an office and store was completed. In the same year, the newly independent Ghana Ministry of Education, which at the time was embarking a vigorous universal education program, formally took responsibility for the teachers' salaries and other expenses. The day to day management remained with the local board of directors. Thus was established a middle school that my sources described as 'the pride of Botoku.' Further enhancing this pride was the fact that graduating students from the school went on to work in a wide range of occupations across the country and beyond. A former female student, at the time of this study, had recently been elected into the national parliament and appointed a minister in the ruling government. They were hoping to use her influence to lobby the government to have their 18km dirt road sealed at last.

During the course of my research, an enthusiastic source succeeded in locating a list of 19 Botoku citizens from Akyem and Kwahu, areas of the present day Eastern Region of Ghana, who had contributed money to the school project. As I studied the list, I was given a bird's eye view, not only of the types of places Botoku people were migrating to, but also the high heterogeneity of their occupations and social conditions. My first insight was that people were not just migrating to urban areas, but also to other rural towns and villages, some of which were even smaller and more remote than Botoku, to work as farm labourers on the expanding cocoa farms. Second, more men (14) than women (5), as I suspected, were migrating, at least to these Akyem and Kwahu rural communities. Third, people generally appeared happy to pay according to their earning capacity. The highest contributions on the list came from two brothers, each of whom paid 15 British pounds. They were both bricklayers; one of them was also instrumental in constructing the bridges during the 1930s road building. The next highest contribution on the list was a *tro tro* (passenger truck) owner-operator who contributed ten pounds. On the other end of the spectrum were men and women engaged in low paying labouring tasks and small scale road side trades. These people clearly did not have as much to give but were happy to contribute one pound, ten shillings or even five shillings. The total contribution on the list amounted to 61 pounds and ten shillings.

The story was told that, on several occasions, the people travelling round the country collecting the levies tried in vain to discourage some Botoku people from contributing money, because of their apparent dire financial circumstances. But this was flatly rejected because, no matter how poor they were, everybody, as Ewe people say, wanted at least a little of their oil to be in the dish; meaning everyone wanted to be part of the process. The sense of achievement in establishing the middle school is all the more important when one considers that no more than two percent of the African population had access to primary school education during the period when Ghana became independent, which was the same time that the school opened.

Unlike the 1930s road building, in which every able-bodied Botoku citizen participated, one of the seven Botoku clan groups did not participate in the middle school project. As in most parts of Eweland, the formation of political parties leading to Ghana becoming an independent nation, sharply divided the Botoku community along party lines. For Ewe people living under the British mandated territory, the issue was whether to join the British Gold Coast and become part of modern Ghana, or to join their Ewe-speaking brothers and sisters under the French mandated territory to become a united Togoland. While support of united Ghana won the ensuing UN plebiscite of 1956, those who wanted a united Togo soon evolved into a secessionist movement. The newly independent Ghana government, under Kwame Nkrumah, saw this as a threat to the territorial integrity of the new nation. Under Nkrumah's notorious preventive detention act, anyone professing unification with Togo was detained indefinitely and without trial. To escape this draconian act many Ewe secessionist leaders and chiefs went into self-imposed exile in Togo, with some of them, quite ironically, living in close proximity to Notsie where centuries before, their ancestors had escaped Agorkoli's tyrannical rule.

The clan chief whose people did not participate in the middle school project was one of many Botoku people who took sanctuary in Togo at the time. The story went that, for several years this chief, a strong supporter of unification with Togo, and the paramount chief who strongly favoured a united Ghana, had not been on speaking terms. The conflict, many people felt, was disrupting the traditionally cohesive Botoku community. In response, the same groups of non-resident educated elite who championed the building of the middle school, took it upon themselves to reconcile the differences between the paramount and the clan chief, a successful resolution marked by a public celebration and peace rituals. The two warring chiefs and the entire community were reminded of the old saying that when two elephants fight it is the grass that suffers. In other words, the community expected them as leaders to look beyond their egos by putting their differences aside for the greater good. The roles of the non-resident elites in providing leadership and support for the middle school, combined with their conflict mediation roles, would henceforth legitimize non-residents as key players, if not lead players, in the development of the ancestral village.

This chapter has shown that, traditionally, most West African societies relied on forms of cooperative labour for the provision of public amenities. All able-bodied people belonging to a village would pool their labour periodically, under the auspices of the chiefs and clan leaders, to construct or maintain public facilities. This included tracks and pathways to the farms and creeks where water was collected, building and maintaining the village gathering or meeting place, as well as organizing fighting forces to protect the village from intruders. British and German colonial authorities used this traditional cooperative labour system for their own purposes. Through the infamous forced labour policies, villages periodically provided people to work on colonial infrastructure systems, including railway and road building, as well as carrying colonial officials in hammocks.

As the next chapter will show, independent Ghanaian governments, since 1957, have also utilized the same communal labour principles as the basis for enabling communities to build social amenities. Under these policies, any village or community of people wanting to build public utilities, such as schools, roads, post offices, health centres, etc., would need to provide their own labour and materials, while the government provided the technical expertise. Perhaps more importantly, the next chapter will show that, except for Nkrumah's draconian laws against Ewe unification around the time of independence, which drove many Ewe chiefs and supporters of united Eweland into exile in neighbouring Togo towns and villages, political independence, combined with effective traditional governance, did bring Botoku an uninterrupted peace and stability, free of overt external pressures, for the first time in its history. The way this relative stability allowed the community to build upon and consolidate the long tradition of self-help projects in partnership with government is the subject of the next chapter.

18 km dirt road

Honourable Akua Dansua (former pupil of the middle school) with Kofi Annan

Togbe Tamtia V as young chief, 1950s

Public Peace ritual after major conflict

Water Hand Pumps, Health Clinic, Electrification and *Fiasa* (chief's 'palace') from 1970s to 2000s

In this chapter, I build on the story of the road and middle school projects discussed in the previous chapter, by examining four other discrete community infrastructure initiatives undertaken from the 1970s through to the 2000s. These include hand pump wells in the 70s; a clinic in the 80s; electrification in the 90s; and a three-room *fiasa* or 'palace' for the paramount chief in 2004/2005. Besides illustrating the wide variety of physical infrastructure projects that fall under the rubric of community development, I also wish to make three specific points.

Unlike the road and school projects discussed in the previous chapter, where clearly identified development elites (pioneer cash-croppers in the 1930s and nascent teaching elite in the 1950s) were the originators, there were no special interest groups behind these later projects. And, unlike the colonial policy environment, which was at best indifferent and at worst hostile to local micro community development, there was a much more supportive and indeed, partnership approach to development during the post independent period, irrespective of the political and ideological persuasion of the ruling government. Another point to be made is the formalization of the emergent dual governance structure for the purposes of managing development projects. On the one hand, the traditional hereditary chiefs and elders had leadership in helping the community at large decide their development priorities. On the other, a non-remunerated, often educated and technical, project management committee was appointed to oversee the practical logistics of planning and implementing the project, while the chiefs and elders remained in the background to help enforce the decisions of the project management committees.

Botoku, according to my sources, is richly endowed with creeks and water holes, from which the people had always gathered water for domestic use. Indeed, it was the abundant water resources that partially motivated their migrating ancestors to make a permanent home on the land in the first place. While water from creeks and water holes like Kpe and Atsave were used mainly for washing, others like Axotoe, Avatu and Nomadoe were reserved solely for drinking because of their special tastes. Over time, and especially since the adoption of corrugated iron roofing, first by pioneer cocoa growers and tradesmen from the 1920s and later by salaried elites, mainly teachers from the 40s, most households harvested and stored small quantities of rainwater to supplement their traditional supplies. Unlike some of their neighbouring towns and villages, such as Vapko, Botoku creeks and water holes, for reasons nobody knew, never contained guinea worms; a common and debilitating source of water-borne infections in many parts of West Africa at the time. The people were generally happy and proud of their water sources, which until recently were revered deities and hence well maintained environmentally. The problem, according to them, came during the unusual and prolonged dry seasons, when some of the creeks and water holes simply dried out, or yielded limited amounts of water.

The increasingly erratic and unreliable weather patterns, some believed, had to do with the construction of the Akosombo hydroelectric dam in the 60s. This, the largest artificially created lake in the world, inundated large tracks of their rainforests and other farming, hunting and sacred grounds. Stories were told of women and children, who had responsibility for collecting water for household use, spending large amounts of time going further and further away from the village to obtain water. Most of these women and children would get up as early as the first cockcrow (3.00-4.00am), when it was still very dark, so they could be among the first to reach the water sources. In a region endowed with some of the most venomous reptiles and other creatures, snake, scorpion and other poisonous bites were not uncommon. But it was not just the physical hazards my story-tellers were keen to emphasize.

Like most Ewes, and indeed Ghanaians and Africans generally, Botoku people strongly believe the world around them was filled with all sorts of spirits, including the ghosts of dead people. For the people of Botoku, there are two types of death. There is a good death, and there is a bad death. A good death occurs when a person dies of old age, or after a protracted illness from which everyone agrees there is little chance of recovering. A bad death on the other hand, occurs when a person, especially in the prime of life, dies suddenly without any obvious signs of illness, through accident or in childbirth. Just as the grieving families find it harder to come to terms with a bad death, so too, the victims find it hard to accept. The *tsiami* (spokesperson) of one of my research groups narrated a story to illustrate the point. A tall, beautiful woman with a wonderful singing voice, and popular member of the local *bobobo* dance group, probably in her late 30s, died in child birth (about 1970). It was her second birth and this child, like the first, survived. The entire village was devastated. The dead woman herself, they believed, was equally devastated because she was a person who loved life and adored children and would not accept not having the opportunity to bring up her own two little children. Her death occurred during one of the great prolonged dry seasons, when the nearby creeks and water sources yielded very little water.

One day a group of children got up early to collect water before heading off to school. On the way they heard a beautiful sweet voice singing a *bobobo* (a local popular music) song but they did not see anyone. When they arrived at the water hole they saw a woman, robed in white, who was sitting beside her water pot. Because it was typically dark during this early morning task, and despite the aid of their lanterns, it was not easy for early risers to recognize people by face and so people tended to identify each other by voice. The first of the group of young people to fill his bucket asked the woman in the white robe to help him lift his filled bucket onto his head. Suddenly, in a nasal voice apparently characteristic of ghosts, the woman said she was sorry she couldn't help because termites had eaten the flesh of her arms after her burial. Suddenly, all the school children recognized the voice, despite the nasal intonation, as that of the attractive and popular woman who had died. Frightened, the children threw their water pots and buckets away and ran back to the village to report their encounter. The relevance of these stories was to highlight how dire, and often disruptive, the water situation could be for Botoku people, especially during prolonged dry seasons. This is why when Togbega (paramount chief), received a letter from Ho (regional capital) that the government planned to dig artesian wells for rural villages to ensure water was available all year round, the idea was accepted with great alacrity.

The story was told how, the same day the letter arrived, Togbega asked his *kpodola* (town crier) to sound the gong gong summoning the whole village to a meeting the following morning so the contents of the letter could be discussed. Although the government with development aid from DANIDA (Danish International Development Agency) was willing to drill and install hand pumps on the wells, those present at the meeting were informed that each village had to meet certain conditions in order to be eligible for the water project. First, each community had to be willing to provide communal labour during the drilling and installment of the pumps. Second, each participating community had to raise funds to support local residents to be trained in pump maintenance at Ho. These people would then return to the village to take responsibility for servicing the pumps. Third, each village had to be prepared to raise minimal revenue from the water, partly to pay those servicing the pumps, as well as buy spare parts for maintenance.

No one at the meeting was opposed to the idea so a water committee was formed there and then. They were charged with the responsibility to plan and implement the project, in collaboration with government officials responsible for the rural water program at the regional capital of Ho. Residents provided communal labour, as well as made small monetary contributions, while special letters of appeal, signed by Togbega himself, were sent to all Botoku citizens living outside the village, requesting support. Two people, a young man and woman, were supported by the village to undergo the pump technician training course.

A total of six artesian wells were drilled with lever hand pumps installed on them for drawing the water. Despite overwhelming support and enthusiasm for the water project, most Botoku people, according to my sources, treated the 'pipe' water as it came to be called, at least initially, as supplementary, rather than a replacement for their traditional creeks and water holes. Some people did not like the taste of the 'pipe' water, preferring to drink water from their favourite traditional sources. Others believed there was too much salt in the pipe water and hence would not use it to wash clothing and other materials. High quantities of soap were required to make this water lather and they considered this wasteful.

Today, the pipe water has become the main source of water for the entire village, supplemented by other sources including plastic drinking water sachets sold by private water companies. Various clan groups are responsible for maintaining the pumps that serve their section of the village. At the time of this research, the *Asafoatse* (warrior leader) of the Lobo clan, one of the seven major clan groups, was responsible for looking after the pump located at Lobo. The opening hours for this pump were from about 5.00am to 10.00am and about 4.00pm to 7.00pm. Outside these hours the pump was under padlock so the well would have time to yield water, as well as prevent children playing with the pumps and wasting the water. Five Ghana new pesewa (about 1 US cent) was charged for any head load of water collected from the pipe. The female chief of this clan group was responsible for putting the money collected in a dedicated bank account at the district town, which was then used to maintain the pump. Judging by the long queues of people waiting their turns to fetch water from the various pumps around the village, it was clear a regular and easily accessible water supply remained a challenge for the Botoku community.

Although the clinic project occurred in the 80s, some ten years before this research commenced, there was no consensus among my sources as to how the idea of a clinic came about. Some people believed the idea was copied from the neighbouring Tsrukpe, which had recently built a health post, and so Botoku people became motivated to build their own clinic. Others narrated a very sad story, which they believed was the main catalyst for the decision. According them, a Botoku man was very sick, and his family decided to take him to a hospital at the nearby district town. But, being there were no cars on the 14-km Botoku dirt road, groups of young men volunteered to carry the sick person, by head, to the main motor road at Vakpo where the family could access transport to the hospital. The young people carrying the sick became upset and embarrassed because people in the neighbouring towns, which had easier access to motor vehicles, had mocked and made fun of them, calling them bush and backward people. They were even more revolted by what they considered insensitive and distasteful jokes, when the sick person they had carried passed away shortly after arriving at the hospital.

The young men returned home to report the incident to the chiefs and elders who decided that Botoku needed to have a clinic of their own. Until then most people had no access to any health services, except for the occasional mass inoculation, or when people went to the hospital literally to die because, more often than not, it was too late for the nurses and doctors to help. The young people were convinced that a clinic at Botoku would help families make more informed decisions about the best times to take their sick to the hospital. As usual, Togbe's town crier summoned a village meeting where the issue was discussed at length.

There were no objections to the clinic proposal and a committee of five, including an experienced professional accountant recently retired back to the village, was created. The committee was given responsibility to plan and implement the project on a day to day basis, while the chiefs and elders pledged to remain in the background to support and enforce the committee's decisions. As with the other projects, all residents would provide communal labour and minimal amounts of cash. But the main source of finance for the clinic, they believed, would have to come from the non-resident Botoku people. The committee wrote, on behalf of the chiefs and elders, to key Botoku people living in different parts of the country, asking them to convene meetings of citizens living in their locations to inform them of the clinic project and to collect and send monies to the committee back in Botoku. Letters were also sent to individual Botoku people living in North America and Europe at the time, appealing to them to donate generously to the effort.

A Botoku man who lived outside the village, but was building a house back home, died before the building could be completed. His extended family in the village offered to allow the committee to renovate two rooms in the uncompleted house for use as the clinic but his children, who were all living outside the village at the time, were unhappy about the arrangement. The children had planned to complete the house so they could have a place to lodge whenever they visited the ancestral home, as non-residents frequently did in order to attend funerals, festivals and other family obligations. Luckily, the government had only recently built a total of 40 houses for families of flood victims whose land was inundated by the lake. One of those houses belonged to the paramount chief's family, and so he offered the two-room house as the site of the clinic.

Three young people were trained in community nursing and first aid at Ho at the expense of the community and were to come back after their training to run the clinic. In the meantime, Botoku people living in Ho and other places, also lobbied ministry of health authorities to support the clinic. As well as financial contributions, prominent Botoku people donated quantities of medicine and medical equipment towards the clinic.

After four years of resource mobilization and lobbying, the Ministry of Health assumed responsibility and posted two nursing staff (unfortunately not those trained by the community) to run the clinic, which was officially opened in 1984 by the Minister. In 2005, under its rural health scheme, the government built a new health post (costing some 50,000 cedis or 5,000 US dollars), to replace the existing clinic. My research participants reflected that Botoku residents were always willing to take part in communal labour, because they knew heaven helped those who helped themselves. The same group also reflected that levies collected by the clinic committee were well used. There was rarely talk of money being misused or people fighting over resources, as was so common with development projects funded by NGOs (non-government organizations).

Anything relating to health, (such as weighing babies, immunization, HIV, malaria and cholera education), they argued, must first go to the elders and the clinic committee. Togbega (paramount chief) then summoned the town crier to call a meeting for all those concerned, so the information could be presented and discussed. No matter what the issue, custom demanded Togbega summon everyone to the meeting ground to have their say. It was up to the person bringing the idea to then convince people the idea was a good one. Although Botoku was proud of their new health post, it was still hard for people to access health services, both at the health post and the district hospitals, because of user-pay services introduced as part of World Bank/ IMF structural adjustment policies from the 1980s. Despite government subsidies for some essential health services, patients had to make a co-payment plus pay for medications. This remained a major barrier to people accessing services in a timely fashion. Two incidents, both of which occurred at the time of this research, were used to illustrate their point.

A woman contracted a group of young men to clear a piece of land for her, in preparation for establishing a new farm. The young men went to start the work early in the day, before the tropical heat became unbearable, while the woman followed later with food for the labourers to eat. On her way, she was bitten by a snake she believed was a cobra, very close to the farm at about 9.00am. The young men responded to her call by first applying some herbal treatment, and then carrying her on their heads, a distance of about 4km, back to the village. The clinic, which did not have anti-venom drugs, advised the family to take the woman to the district hospital. Since there was no cash readily available to go the hospital, the woman was taken to a traditional healer across the road from the clinic for therapy, while they looked around for money to go to the hospital. At about 4.00pm money was finally secured and the woman taken to hospital, only to die on arrival before treatment could begin.

On another occasion, a mother left her sick daughter, who was in her 20s, at the district hospital following a diagnosis, so she could raise funds from families back at Botoku, which had to be paid before treatment could proceed. By the following morning when she returned with the money, the daughter had already passed away. Access to basic health services clearly remained a barrier for most people, and my informants hoped the current national health insurance scheme, aimed to provide coverage for essential services and drugs, would go some way towards improving the situation.

Ghana undertook a major hydroelectric project in the 1960s, as part of the industrialization policy of the newly independent country (Chambers, 1970). As with many post colonial countries embarking on national development programs at the time, the loans to fund the hydroelectric project came from the Bretton Woods international finance institutions of World Bank and International Monetary Fund (IMF) charged with post WWII economic recovery. These were mainly focused in war ravaged Europe but later would assist newly independent countries with nation building. Although the hydroelectric project was successful in supplying energy to the nascent industrial sector and urban households, a significant proportion of the energy was exported to nearby countries to generate the foreign currency required for repaying the loans.

This meant rural dwellers such as Botoku, whose lands had been inundated as a result of the dam construction, were literally and metaphorically kept in the dark. This was all the more frustrating considering rural people living close to international borders with countries, such as Togo, could see the high tension power lines carried above their heads to these places. As with most Ghanaian rural dwellers, the Botoku people's message to successive governments since the 1960s was a need to extend the hydroelectric power to rural communities. This made the electrification project by far the most ambitious and longest project in terms of the duration it took to lobby, plan and implement. But, the research participants were careful to point out that the electrification project was more than just access to electricity for lighting. For them, the story behind the electricity project was one of capacity to sacrifice and adapt to changing circumstances.

Ever since their permanent settlement, they argued, the Botoku people had looked towards their Akan-speaking Kwahu and Akyem cousins (across the Volta to the west) for economic sustenance (because of the abundant land and trade opportunities) along the river, rather than their Ewe speaking brothers and sisters east of the Volta. The extent of the relationships was manifested in such institutions as chieftaincy, Akan names resulting from inter-marriage, the lyrics of sacred songs and oaths, as well as drum language. Most Botoku families, to this day, had family ties dating back more than 100 years in Kwahu and Akyem towns and villages, because of the strong economic links to the Volta river basin. But all that changed drastically with the construction of the Volta River hydroelectric dam, which inundated large tracks of their farming, hunting and sacred lands. A traditionally agrarian people, fishing was never part of their way of life, and hence all the promises from government that there would be an opportunity for people to fish rather than cultivating the land, meant very little to them at the time. For many Botoku people, and indeed many others living in the Volta basin, the Volta was a powerful deity. These people simply did not believe any human being was capable of building a dam to stop the water from flowing down stream.

The story was told of a renowned Botoku medicine man living near a fishing community close to the Volta. He maintained a popular shrine for the Volta river god patronized by many people seeking protection from bad spirits and for good fortune in life. With the frequent publicity campaigns, mostly through the popular transistor radio, warning those living near the Volta about the impending floods, people flocked to the medicine man's shrine to consult the river god as to whether the flood would affect their farms and settlements. Apparently, each divination resulted in the same message from the oracle. The river god wanted to reassure people that the proposed dam would never eventuate because no human being, not even socialist atheist president Kwame Nkrumah (who openly said that he neither believed in Christian nor African gods), was able to stop the water from their most revered, and indeed feared, river flowing downstream. Because of skepticism by a deeply religious population, some people did not take the government warnings about the impending floods seriously until it was too late. As it turned out, the renounced healer, like many of the people consulting him, woke up one morning to discover that his huts, crops and livestock, and indeed his beloved and popular shrine, were half submerged in water.

But the impact of the floods, my sources said, was not just limited to those living in close proximity to the Volta. The entire Botoku community had to make severe adjustments, probably not experienced in their history since the time their ancestors left Notsie. But, like their ancestors, Botoku was always willing to sacrifice and adapt to changing circumstances. The story of how government acquired land to build the small township of 40 dwellings for flood victims adjoining the Botoku village was used to illustrate one dimension of the extent of the sacrifice they had to make. The most suitable land for the resettlement happened to be sacred; the cemetery where people who died accidental or bad deaths were buried. The ghosts of such people could be troublesome and hence their burial grounds were highly sacred. Stories were told of how unsuspecting victims entering the cemetery sometimes heard the voices of people talking without seeing anyone, or stones that were thrown at people entering the burial grounds for no apparent reason. Several sheep, goats and large quantities of alcoholic drink (some of my sources admitted these were provided by government) had to be used for ritual purposes, in order to pacify the dead before the sacred

71

cemetery was successfully relocated to make room for the resettlement township.

While some of the resettled were Botoku citizens, a larger proportion were non-citizens. The result was that, within a relatively short period of time, Botoku had to absorb people from virtually every part of Ghana. Although some of these people returned to live closer to the lake once the flooding ceased, others became an integral part of the Botoku community. The point of all these stories, is to emphasize how unhappy they had been that, despite all the destruction and the sacrifice they had to make as a result of the hydroelectric project, like most rural communities, they had not benefited from the power. This was a message repeated for every government official visiting Botoku over the next 20 years. Eventually it became government policy to extend the light to rural areas, especially settlements nearer the lake whose lands were affected. But, these residents were required to take the initiative and purchase their own poles, and provide communal labour, while the government provided equipment and technical support.

Botoku citizens living at Ho were the first to hear of this government policy. Two people were sent home to inform the Togbe Tamtia and his elders in 1989. Electrification project committees were set up in Botoku, Ho, Accra and all major towns and cities to mobilize support for the idea and to collect financial contributions from non-residents. As before, Botoku citizens living overseas were all contacted for financial contributions. Special bank accounts were opened at Accra, Ho and Kpandu for the project. Inhabitants at home were levied 3,000 cedis (roughly 3 US dollars), plus required to participate in communal labour. Those residing outside the village added financial contributions ranging from 10,000 to 50,000 cedis (10 to 50 US dollars), determined according to their ability. The Accra committee bought and transported home the first ten poles out of an expected total of 90 in March 1991 when the project was formally launched.

Electrification meetings took place in Accra and other main towns on the last Sunday of the month, which was immediately after the monthly payday for salaried and hourly wage earners throughout Ghana. People came to the meetings to pay whatever they could afford in the month towards their levies. The meetings were also a time to see family and friends. After ten years of stop-start-stop, electricity finally arrived, with fan fare and celebrations, at Botoku in 2000. Although people sometimes complained about communal labour and financial contributions, there was also a general acceptance, according to my sources, that development projects had other intrinsic values; for one they broke down barriers and brought people together as community. Those living outside the village believed, without development projects, their children would be lost. Development projects and attendance at funerals gave young people born or living outside Botoku an understanding of where they came from. What was the alternative in today's world? Alcohol and wee (marijuana)? Not knowing who you are? The more young people gave of themselves to their community, they concluded, the more they got out of it.

The fourth and final physical infrastructure project discussed (a *fiasa* (palace) for the paramount chief) was important because, despite the increasing partnership or support from government for their development initiatives, it was reassuring that, like the road building in the 1930s, Botoku still had the capacity to initiate and undertake projects of their own accord, without government support. The story behind the building of the *fiasa* was also significant though, because it shows how technology, and in this particular case, the availability of rural electrification, can dramatically change age-old customs and traditions for better or worse. Midway through this research project in 2004, Togbe Tamtia V, paramount chief of Botoku since 1951, died at the age of 92. My sources described him as an enlightened and forward looking chief under whose leadership Botoku experienced 50 years of largely uninterrupted peace and stability, underpinned by strong communal norms of what is good and right and what is wrong. This kind of uninterrupted leadership and relative peace, free from external pressures to dominate, was probably unknown to Botoku people since their ancestors escaped from Notsie. As a result, despite rural isolation and poverty, Botoku achieved significant improvements in their material, social and spiritual living conditions which development, or the search for a better future, was all about. The deceased paramount chief was well known and respected by his peers throughout the district, and so many chiefs wished to attend his burial to pay their last respects. Besides this influx, as custom demanded, all the six sister towns and villages would be descending on Botoku for the chief's burial rituals, expected to go on for eight days.

The main problem facing the Botoku community was that they lacked a decent *fiasa*, or palace, befitting the standing of the departed chief. The idea of building a palace was nothing new. Botoku people had considered building one over the years, but had to set the idea aside in order to make room for other more pressing priorities such as schools, clinics, markets, roads etc. The death of this well-regarded chief, whose long reign everyone agreed had been a potent force for development, was seen as opportunity for Botoku to finally build a *fiasa* as part of the elaborate preparations required to honour him. For some, a new palace would also serve as incentive for an incoming paramount chief, since it was becoming harder and harder to find appropriate and legitimate contenders willing to accept the role. This is partly because Botoku people generally consider being a chief too much responsibility and too restrictive. There are a wide range of things a chief can or cannot do, such as not socializing, drinking, or eating in public. Moreover, unlike their Akan cousins across the Volta, Botoku had very little dedicated stool lands. These were lands from which incumbent chiefs could use timber, oil palm and other resources to meet the growing expenses associated with the office. Christianity was also complicating the situation because people of faith were not willing to become chiefs due to the elaborate rituals associated with the office, which most considered too pagan.

While the majority supported the palace proposal, a vocal minority was said to be opposed to the idea. The 'opponents' of the palace were not against building the palace itself though. They were opposed to the idea of keeping the dead chief's corpse in a morgue until such time that a palace was built so it could then be laid in state for a befitting burial. Those opposing the palace agreed that, like most Ghanaians, funerals were very important for Botoku people. Funerals were a time to give support for the bereaved, celebrate life, and for the community to renew itself and heal. Because a funeral was such an important event, it was traditionally organized to give adequate time for every member of the extended families and friends to be able to attend. Traditionally, when a person dies, the corpse is buried within three days. Thereafter, an appropriate and more convenient future date is set for the actual funeral rites to occur. One of the unintended and bizarre consequences of rural electrification in Ghana was that the energy, which many believed would promote cottage industries, rather, spawned the proliferation of morgues all over the country, with an increasing tendency by families to keep corpses from anything between weeks to more than one year in order to adequately prepare for the funeral.

To the opponents of the palace, keeping a corpse in a morgue for such lengthy periods of time was not just financially wasteful, but the long wait before burial rites were performed could also be psychologically distressful for the immediate families. So long as their beloved ones remained unburied, it would be hard for them to have a sense of closure. In the end, a compromise was struck. The palace would be built and all citizens would contribute towards it. Those opposed to keeping the corpse until the palace was completed were free, as they demanded, not to contribute money towards the mortuary fees, so long as they contributed toward the palace itself. A prominent Botoku businessman donated 50 bags of cement to kick start the project, which as usual was undertaken mainly through combinations of communal labour and small monetary contributions by residents, plus fundraising from non-residents. It took nearly one year to complete the three-room palace. At its completion, it was the site of an elaborate eight-day burial ritual, enacting both the sad memories and tribulations of the past, but also celebrating the achievements and triumphs.

At the time of finalizing this book, five years since the burial of the previous chief, there was still an acting chief in charge of the overall governance of Botoku while the search for the substantive paramount chief continues. Again this is partly because of the difficulty of getting capable candidates willing to take on the responsibility, and partly because of the high financial costs involved in installing a new chief. In the next chapter, I examine some of the ways in which the Botoku people have used culture, especially customs and traditions about death and funeral rites, to legitimize and ensure citizen participation in development projects.

Hand pump for water

Asafos enacting the past

Late Togbe Tamtia V

Chapter 7

Culture as a Two-Edged Sword

For Botoku people, development was not just about physical infrastructure projects as in roads, schools, markets and clinics. Development was also about the customs and traditions that guide social interactions between people with regards to right and wrong behaviour and the capacity to ensure, as much as possible, that citizens or members of the society, no matter their social standing, abide by the relevant social and cultural norms and expectations. Customs and traditions thus enhance social order, stability and community cohesion, all of which are essential prerequisites for any meaningful development to occur. But the same traditions and customs can often, quite ironically, undermine the dignity and well-being of people, especially the vulnerable sections of the community, if approached or applied uncritically.

This makes culture, particularly in the context of traditionally-oriented societies experiencing rapid social change, in my view, a double-edged sword. Depending on how people, and more so those in positions of authority, understand and use culture, it can either promote or undermine development. Consequently, an important focus for development efforts, I believe, ought to be the creation of safe environments for respectful but critical conversations among communities of people with regards to their underlying customs and traditions. The goal of these conversations is to identify aspects relevant to the challenges and opportunities of contemporary living conditions, and hence worth preserving. The second part, of course, is identifying those clearly obsolete or redundant, and accordingly in need of being dismissed.

In this chapter, I examine three broad categories of Botoku people's recent attempts to adapt some of their age-old customs and traditions in line with changing circumstances, and some of the challenges and opportunities involved. Included in the case studies are: a 1970s decision to make citizen participation in community development projects a condition for the chiefs and elders performing funeral rituals on ancestral land; a 1960s decision not to allow dogs in Botoku due to the threat of a rabies epidemic; and, finally, a 1970s decision to outlaw *akanyiyi* (trial by ordeal) in the case of witchcraft and other sorcery accusations. Through these, I wish to point out the

79

difficulties, but also the windows of opportunity, that may be available for development workers and researchers to fully engage with and, hopefully, help change cultural practices and traditions. Ideally this will apply even to the most sensitive areas found to be inimical to the dignity and well-being of the people with whom they work. This, I believe, should be an important part of the quest for development, particularly in traditionally –oriented societies experiencing rapid social change, as in the case of many African countries and other developing nations.

Over two-thirds of the estimated 10,000 Botoku citizens live and work outside the ancestral village. For Botoku residents, the frequent demand for communal labour and attendance at development meetings can exert a great deal of pressure on a busy agrarian people. For the non-residents, expected to pay taxes towards the provision of public amenities in their adopted place of residence, a development levy back in their native village constitutes an additional burden, especially for those with a lower income. Many of the people living outside and classified as non-residents may have spent almost all of their adult lives away from the village. Some of the younger generation may even have been born outside the village. Yet, most of these people, including people like myself and my children living in Australia, continue to be regarded as citizens, expected to contribute our fair share to any communal self-help initiatives.

What makes the community development spirit and expectation so durable and adaptable over the years? Is it love for one's ancestral village? Is it the resiliency and adaptability of the traditional chieftaincy governance systems? Or is it the intrinsic value of social connectedness (people building trusting relationships with each other) that arises from working together to achieve a common purpose? All of these may be contributing factors. However, one critical factor not always obvious to the outside observer was the role belief systems and cultural practices about life and death played in maintaining and reproducing the communal self-help spirit. As I pondered these questions during the course of my research, an incident occurred which gave me clues to the answer.

An extended family member of mine living in Accra had died and so I suspended all planned interviews in order to join in a family meeting convened to prepare for the arrival of the corpse for funerals. The first question posed by the head of the family at the meeting was whether the deceased had discharged her development obligations, to which the person who had brought the news of the death replied 'yes', and that they had already checked her records from the Accra branch of the development committee. I became curious and at the first interview opportunity following the funeral, I began exploring the links between funerals and development levies at length.

Apparently, at the public meeting when the committee was formed to oversee the clinic project (previous chapter), a participant at the meeting asked the newly established clinic committee what they would do if a Botoku person refused to participate in the project. The committee members responded that they would refer the person to the chiefs and elders for punishment. Not satisfied with the answer, the person asking the question turned to *Togbega* (paramount chief) himself and his elders with the same question: what would they do if a Botoku person refused to participate? After a very long deliberation the *tsiami* (spokesperson) for the chiefs and elders announced their sanction against those who, for no good reason, refused to participate. When a person who refused to participate died, or an immediate family member of the person died, they, the chiefs and elders, the custodians responsible for overseeing funeral rituals, would withhold the performance of those customs until the family paid any development arrears owed by that person.

As it turned out, a Botoku man living outside the village and noted for his apathy and indifference to community improvement initiatives did die during the course of the clinic project. His children, all born and living outside the village, brought their father's corpse back to the ancestral home for funerals. On arrival in the village the chiefs and elders ordered the corpse stay in the vehicle carrying it until all the adult children of the dead paid any development levies owed by themselves, as well as those owed by their late father. If they failed to do so, the children were free to go ahead with burial but they, the chiefs and elders, would not play their ritual roles. Ever since that incident, it became the tradition in Botoku that when a citizen died, whether resident or non-resident, any outstanding development commitments owed by the deceased, or their close relatives, were required to be settled before funeral rites could take place.

As with many Ghanaian and African societies a person's funeral was the most important event in their life. Death, according to my informants, was like *ayatsi* or a sudden tropical storm leaving trails of destruction in its wake. No matter how careful people were, there was never the opportunity to fully take in and appreciate the gathering clouds or warning signs signaling the advent of *ayatsi* before the windy storms took their toll on the roofs and crops of unsuspecting victims. It all happened suddenly and left one wondering whether it was real. But death, like *ayatsi,* was also a time when families and indeed whole villages, stepped back and took stock of their situation. It was a time they mobilized all the available material, emotional and spiritual resources of the entire community in support of the bereaved.

The point my sources were trying to make, was that withholding community support for a person's funeral was probably the most serious sanction a Botoku person, whether living or dead, could expect. Although more than half of Botoku citizens reside outside the village, like most of their Ghanaian counterparts, these non-resident citizens, for the most part, maintain strong attachments to the ancestral village and return several times a year for funerals, festivals and other family reasons. Custom required, for example, that no matter where a citizen died, the body be buried back on the ancestral lands. Even if burial occurred elsewhere, funeral rites were still to be performed in the village. This, according to my sources, was to enable the spirit of the dead person to enter the ancestral world. Failure to observe proper funeral rites for the dead resulted in the spirit not being able to settle. For those who no longer believed in ancestral spirits, or considered the cost of transporting bodies over long distances for burial on ancestral lands an unnecessary waste of scarce resources, they still valued funeral rites in the native village as a form of healing and closure for family and friends back in the village. Even those diaspora who did not want their corpses returned to the ancestral village because of the costs involved, were still adamant in taking part in symbolic rituals. For example, pieces of hair, finger and toe nails were taken back for symbolic burial and funeral rites to take place so the extended family back home could have closure, heal their grief and move on emotionally.

Despite Christianity, education and other outside influences, the belief in funeral rites on ancestral lands remained remarkably strong, not only among the Botoku people, but other Ghanaians more broadly. I will use a personal experience to further illustrate the pervasiveness of the practice. In 1999, after I began the research for this book, I relocated from the central Australian desert town of Alice Springs to Townsville in north Queensland to take a new job, as well as to live in a tropical climate more similar to southern Ghana. On the first day I reported to my new job, located behind a large teaching hospital, I saw a woman sitting under a tree nearby. We instantly recognized each other as Ghanaians because of the clothes we wore. After exchanging greetings she explained she lived in Papua New Guinea

(PNG) with her husband and children, but had come to Townsville the previous week with her husband who had been referred to the hospital for a serious health condition. I visited the man at the hospital a couple of times that week, and we discovered I went to boarding school with one of his cousins at Akropong in the eastern region. By the weekend, I received a phone call from the woman that her husband had passed away and so, together with the other few Africans in our community, we met with the woman to work out her options.

One possibility was to take the body back to PNG for the funerals. This was where the family had been living for about fifteen years. The other was to let the children and close friends in PNG come to Townsville, and for the funeral to occur there. Then of course, there was the third option, which was to take the body back to Ghana for burial on ancestral lands, though the expense involved in the latter frightened some of us, to say the least. After several phone calls to the relevant heads of family back in Ghana, the decision was crystal clear; the extended family back in Ghana wanted the body sent back home for burial and funeral rites. So, within a week in a new job, in a new town, I found myself assisting the distraught widow in sorting through the complex logistics and bureaucratic procedures, including dealing with undertakers, immigration and airlines, for the body to be flown back to Ghana.

It was only then it struck me that the corpse of a Botoku man, who had spent over twenty years in North America, had been similarly returned for burial in the ancestral village only a few years previous. Indeed, of all the Botoku people who died during the course of this research between the period 1995 and 2010, whether resident or not, my sources were able to identify only a few instances that, for logistic reasons, the corpses were not brought home for burial, though in each case funeral rituals were performed on ancestral lands. My interest here is not so much the reasons for the deep attachment to burial and funerals on ancestral lands, as a fuller explanation would take another book. The main point I wish to highlight here is that, whether for good or bad, burial or funeral rituals remain a major form of connection to ancestral home in most parts of Ghana. For the Botoku people, the requirement on families to discharge development obligations owed by a deceased as a condition for proper funeral rituals on ancestral lands, harsh and insensitive as it might sound, constituted important tools in the hands of traditional authorities for enforcing social norms, including participation in community self-help activities. Significantly, the fear of invoking such sanctions meant families often exerted pressure on members to discharge their development responsibilities in a timely way so that, in practice, the sanction was rarely invoked.

Similar social controls were used to guard against and prevent misuse of development funds. This was particularly relevant in relatively poor countries such as Ghana, where incomes were, and still are, so low that many development committee members themselves found it hard to survive on their incomes. The relative effectiveness of such traditional social controls at the village level was one reason one rarely hears of corruption or misuse of development funds for private gains, as was often the case with NGO funded projects: the latter lacking the cultural mechanisms of accountability. Interestingly, over the years, the Christian churches also adopted the traditional practice, so that active participation and contribution to church development activities became a condition for church burial. For Botoku people, my sources proudly asserted, even the dead were still called upon to account for their roles and responsibilities as members of society. Culture and, in this particular instance, the importance people attach to funeral rituals on ancestral lands, thus played positive legitimizing roles in citizen participation in development projects.

But culture, as the case of *akanyinyi* (trial by ordeal) as a form of conflict mediation will show, later in this chapter, can also serve to undermine development if applied uncritically. Before examining the *akanyiyi* incident though, let us look at the 1960s decision to remove dogs from Botoku, as another example of the Botoku people's attempts to reform and adapt culture to align with their changing circumstances.

The background for the decision not to allow dogs in Botoku stems from the construction of the Akosombo hydroelectric dam, which, as the previous chapter showed, resulted in the largest manmade lake in the world. The net result was that large tracks of Botoku farming and hunting grounds were flooded. According to my sources, dogs had been an integral part of Botoku people's lives for as long as they could remember, and certainly long before their ancestors embarked on their dramatic and adventurous journey out of Notsie. Stories were narrated to show how, at critical stages of their migratory journeys, clever and obedient dogs, acting almost like humans, played vitally important roles in assisting the reconnaissance or advance parties in detecting and escaping enemy attention. Since their permanent settlement at Botoku, dogs continued to play important hunting and security roles, which was the reason almost every Botoku household kept at least a dog or two. At a time when slave raids were rampant, the knowledge dogs would raise the alarm at the sight of an intruder at night was enough to keep itinerant raiders away from the village. Hence such raiders concentrated their efforts on waylaying unsuspecting individual or small groups of travellers. Dogs also became the best sentinels to sound the alarm warning of colonial officials, long before the visitors actually arrived in the village. This allowed the relevant chiefs and able-bodied people to take to the bush, thus escaping what they believed were the colonial authorities' insatiable demands for forced labour and *lampo* (tax). The point of all of this is that, historically, dogs were indeed Botoku people's closest friends in times of need.

But all that changed in a most dramatic and sad way early one morning in 1967 when a rabid dog went on a rampage, biting two people and several other dogs before it was caught and put down. The two people bitten died, one after the other, within a matter of hours. Togbega (paramount chief) invoked his *Atam* or sacred oath (which he rarely did) forbidding anyone to leave the village for their farms or to travel outside the village to nearby markets until the crisis was fully dealt with and safety restored to the village.

For some people, the sudden deaths were all the work of witches; the sick dog merely the conduit through which the witches wreaked their havoc. The reality was, since much of the land had been flooded by the lake, Botoku people simply did not have as much use for their hunting dogs. As a result many dogs were left largely uncared for, and at the same time, they continued to breed in large numbers. It should be no surprise that there were frequent attacks on people by angry and frustrated dogs. After two long days of public deliberation, during which different arguments and perspectives were put forward (including confirmation from the government veterinary officer from Kpandu that the dog was indeed rabid), the chiefs and elders retreated to consult *abrewa* (a mythical old lady reputed for her wisdom) for advice as to what should happen.

Several hours later the gathering reconvened and the tsiami (spokesperson) narrated *abrewa's* decision. Botoku people were traditionally hunters and so dogs had always been an important part of their life. Since water from the lake took their lands people no longer had any use for hunting dogs. The days when dogs were needed to keep away intruding slave raiders, and to sound the warning of visiting colonial authorities had also gone. Uncared for but continuing to breed, there was a real chance the tragedy that had befallen the village could happen again. Under the circumstances, *abrewa's* considered view was that, beginning from that day, everyone had one month to take their dogs to friends or families in other villages where dogs were still valued for hunting. Any dog found in Botoku after the one month grace period would immediately be put down. Since then it has been the custom not to allow dogs into Botoku.

Looking back nearly forty years since that sad and dramatic decision was taken, I asked my research participants to use hindsight to consider whether things might have been handled differently. Several observations were brought forward. Once hunting was no longer a viable activity for Botoku people, it was hard to see any future for dogs in the village because most people simply did not have the means to care for dogs as pets. The most difficult part of the decision for people was the strong emotional attachment they had to their dogs. Once the community came to terms with and accepted that change was inevitable however, they began appreciating new opportunities that arose from the decision. For example, Botoku quickly developed a proud reputation as a clean and tidy place where there were no dog droppings, as was often the case in nearby villages. Although sad and even unfair to the dogs at the time, people valued the prompt and decisive nature with which the community leaders dealt with the situation. This, the quick resolution of the crisis, was a major reason people accepted the change so readily.

With the passage of time this custom became much more flexible and accommodating of special needs, albeit under stringent conditions. Nearly forty years after dogs were removed from Botoku, a non-resident couple approached the chiefs and elders for permission to bring their pet dog with them to the village where they were returning to spend their retirement years. The couple, a retired university academic and a retired midwife, had always kept pet dogs and so the elders believed they had the means to care for their dog. Besides, their large fenced property where they would keep the dog was situated at the outskirts of the village. The couple was allowed to bring the dog back on the condition it stayed primarily within their compound and was kept on lead when outside of the property. This concession made this dog, at the time of writing this book, the only dog in Botoku. The important lesson here is that culture is created to serve particular needs in place and time. As a result, it is important to leave the door open for the possibility of cultural change, so long as proper and transparent processes are followed.

The final, and probably the most difficult and divisive category of cultural reforms with which Botoku had to come to terms in recent times, was *akanyinyi,* or trial by ordeal, for those accused of witchcraft and sorcery.

For Botoku people, there were three broad, often overlapping, domains of conflict mediation, which ought to be properly understood in order to place the community dispute over *akanyinyi* in perspective. First, there were conflicts and crimes involving the material or physical domain of the human experience, as in property theft, where all parties to the conflict were clearly identifiable and willing to accept responsibility. This type of conflict required *afemenunya,* or wisdom from tradition, for humans to mediate satisfactorily. Second, there were conflicts involving the material or physical domain of human experience, again as in property theft, but where one party, often the perpetrator, denied or refused to accept responsibility for their action. In such conflicts there may be no choice but to defer to the spirit world for what they believed was instant justice. Third, there were conflicts that squarely belonged to the spirit world such as with accusations of witchcraft and sorcery. Such conflicts were best dealt with by the spirit world through divination and other oracle consultations. For all three domains of conflict, the desire to arrive at the truth of what actually happened, to restore justice, restitution, healing and forgiveness were the main goals of mediation.

Unlike Anglo-Saxon or Westminster legal traditions where responsibility for proving guilt lies with the victim, assisted by the prosecutor plus technicalities of the law, the Botoku system of conflict mediation relies largely on simply arriving at the *anukware* (truth). The truth must come out so those involved: victim, perpetrator and their families, can heal. This process was believed fundamental to any meaningful search for development. What follows is a detailed exploration of the three main domains or spheres of conflict mediation and management, with an aim of examining how world views and belief systems impact development.

First, there are conflicts involving the human domain of experience, where both victim and perpetrator are clearly identified. For such conflicts, an aggrieved party could lodge a complaint with a chief, an elder, or any respected person they believe would have credibility in the eyes of both parties involved. The dispute mediator set a time and invited both parties to attend, reminding them to bring along their respective support people; families or friends. Each party stated their case and the mediator invited questions from the floor for each of the two parties. The mediator then took equal numbers of representatives from the people providing support for the two parties to go and consult *abrewa*, the mythical old lady who, hopefully, would offer a fair and just decision. Very old ladies were traditionally reputed for their wisdom and even-handedness. At *abrewa's* place, often a secluded place to avoid eavesdroppers, this often all-male delegation would begin their deliberation.

The mediator invited each person to take turns and express what they thought should happen. The mediator provided a summary and asked for consensus. If people were happy, then a *tsiami* or spokesperson was appointed for the group. The first task was to role-play how he or she was going to convey *abrewa's* advice convincingly to the waiting audience and the disputants. Others would interject to correct the *tsiami* and the role play narration would continue until everyone visiting *abrewa* was happy the *tsiami* got the story right. The delegation then returned to their seats and the mediator called on the *tsiami* to narrate what *abrewa* had to say about the dispute. The *tsiami,* in an oratory, narrated the story of the dispute; the people involved; what *abrewa* believed happened; how it happened; how both the complainant and defendant and their families must be feeling; who *abrewa* thought was at fault; the sanctions she prescribed; and *abrewa's* advice about what everyone could learn from the incident so it did not happen again in the future.

The punishment for a minor offence might be a simple apology or a bottle of alcohol. More serious offences might warrant fines, alcohol, chicken, or even sheep, to pacify and cleanse the victim or the relevant gods, in cases where taboos and other customs were broken. Those providing support for the guilty person would invariably plead on their behalf for reductions in the fine. A negotiation would ensue, at the end of which the *tsiami* consulted the team who visited *abrewa,* before finally announcing an already pre-determined minimal fine that *abrewa* thought was commensurate with the offence. Where alcohol was part of the fine the alcohol was shared and the first person to be served was the convicted, both to ensure the drink was safe, and also as a face-saving exercise in recognizing it took courage for people to accept they were at fault.

Of course, where one party was not happy, they had the liberty to take the case to another, higher authority. The path might be, for example, from a respected lay person, to a clan head, to one of the seven clan chiefs (either male or female) and finally to the paramount chief. If a person was still unhappy they could then go to the modern magistrate court. I could well relate to these stories for, as a child, I had followed my father to some of these mediation sessions, often harassing him, unsuccessfully, to show me this mythical old lady whom everyone feared and revered so much. But the main point of my sources was how, to this day, the mythical *abrewa's* wisdom accumulated, and over the generations, remained the dominant mechanism for mediating conflicts of this type among Botoku people. It is still only in rare instances that these disputes get to the modern judiciary.

For more serious crimes such as murder, rape, or other violent transgressions within the physical realm of the human experience, more communal strategies were employed. The story of how Botoku traditionally dealt with rape and violence against women was narrated, mainly by my female sources, to illustrate how the communal strategy worked. A woman who suffered an abuse, whether sexual or other physical violence at the hands of a man, would report the incident to the relevant female chief or an elderly woman in the clan. An all-women meeting would be called to evaluate the situation. After explaining what had happened to the gathering, the elderly and most experienced of the women would take turns reminding the younger generation of an age-old Botoku custom of dealing with rape and abuse against women.

An attack on one woman by a single male, the elderly would remind the less experienced, meant an attack on all women by all men, because violence and rape by men did not discriminate between women. If it could happen to one woman, it could happen to any woman. Violence and abuse committed by one man against a woman, the elderly would argue, amounted to no less than a declaration of war by men against women. It was not for nothing that the ancestors, in their wisdom, decided to call *awa awa*, literally meaning the same Ewe word *awa* is used for both penis and war. If for nothing else, the term should serve as reminder to women, and for that matter to men, that the relationship between women and men was a fragile one. It was like a perforated water pot requiring careful handling by everyone, if the water were to be saved for everyone's benefit. Violence by men against women, the argument would continue, meant a total breakdown of trust between women and men.

Under such circumstances, as women, they were left with no choice but to withdraw the most sacred and intimate basis of their relationships with men, namely, sexual intercourse and care for the family. Any Botoku woman violating the prescribed course of action should remember that men had declared war on women, hence they were under attack. Violations on the part of a woman would be interpreted as support for the enemy and hence would be treated as such.

Having laid down the key principles and rationale behind the age-old custom, the women leaders would then outline the dramatic practical course of action. All able-bodied women from puberty and above, would go home and pack the most essential personal items and return immediately to the meeting ground. If a man tried to prevent a woman from packing, the woman was not to argue, but leave everything behind and return immediately to the join the gathering. Except for the breast feeding, no children were allowed to accompany their mothers. From the meeting ground all women would then walk out, literally en masse, to the nearby Tsrukpe village, 6km away, to take asylum with their fellow women there. The leaders would have already notified their nearby Tsrukpe sisters that *awa si* (penis attacked) Botoku women, so their nearby sisters would be expecting them. Once the Botoku women arrived, the Tsrukpe women would billet, feed and care for their sisters. Immediately in such a situation, the conflict ceases to be between an individual male perpetrator of the violence and the female victim.

The conflict or crime now involves three distinct parties, each with their roles and responsibilities. The Botoku women and their Tsrukpe hosts considered themselves wronged or violated by the Botoku men, and so their role was to sit back and wait for restitution and justice, first for the individual female victim of the violence, and second for women in general. The women needed to be pacified, begged, cajoled, and wooed to regain the trust and confidence of their men folks. The second party, the Botoku men, the perpetrators of the violence, had to bring the individual perpetrator to justice by imposing heavy and appropriate fines including money, quantities of alcohol, and several sheep, goats and chicken to fit what would be acceptable to the women. But the Botoku men were not allowed to deal directly with their refugee women folk. All contact between the two must be done through the Tsrukpe chiefs and elders, who assumed the third and final category of roles in the conflict, namely, the mediators and intermediaries. The Botoku men would pass on their fines and prescribed punishment for the perpetrator through their Tsrukpe intermediaries to the women. If the women were satisfied with the fines and punishment, they would accept and return home, but if not, they would reject the offer. The to and fro could go on for days and even weeks before final settlement would be reached. My sources went on at lengths to explain that this age-old custom was only rarely invoked and most people would witness it no more than once or twice in their lifetimes. But the threat of it happening was serious enough, they argued, to act as deterrent against rape and violence against women. It was said the fines associated with the crime were so heavy they could put the perpetrator and their whole extended family into debt for life.

Because both men and women, and indeed the whole village and their Tsrukpe counterparts, were forced to put life on hold for the sake of a crime committed by one individual, this necessarily made the crime everyone's business. As such it was in everyone's interest to frown upon it and hopefully prevent it from happening. This made rape and wife beating such a serious taboo that the individual perpetrator might never fully recover from the stigma and shame associated with the offence. Such customs were highly relevant to the needs and challenges of contemporary Ghana, where rape and violent crimes against women are increasingly treated by the Westminster-based modern judiciary as conflicts between individual victims and the perpetrator. Rather than being considered attacks by all men against all women and hence requiring collective action, they carry less weight.

As one of my female sources concluded, the challenge for both women and men in modern Ghana is how to capitalize on new media, such as group emails, text messages, face books, twitter, and mobile phones. She imagined these resources could put out calls to mobilize women and men at workplaces, neighbouring communities, sporting clubs, within churches, and other clearly identified communities of people, to take direct communal actions against rape and abuse against women. Imagine with her the power that would come from all Asiama or Adabraka (townships in Accra) women, no matter their situation, withdrawing from sexual intercourse and family care for a week, as protest against reported male violence. Add, at the same time, responsible male leaders within these communities rising to the challenge, as the Botoku forebears did, by taking it upon themselves to ensure men and women do right by each other.

The second main category of conflict involved those within the sphere of the material human experience, but for which the perpetrator refused to own up and take responsibility for their actions. For such conflicts the victim would have no choice but to defer to the spirit domain for the *anukware*, or truth, to come out, for justice to be restored and for healing to occur. Here is an example to illustrate how the system works: typically a person steals another person's property, such as crops from the farm, livestock, personal belongings like jewellery, or violates another person as in a sexual assault. The perpetrator refuses to own up to their crime. The victim makes a public announcement, through the village crier, formally putting the perpetrator on notice that unless they own up by a certain deadline, the victim will defer the case to the deity of their choice to handle. If, after the deadline, the perpetrator still refuses to come forward, the victim takes money and alcohol to formally lodge a complaint with a deity.

Retribution by the more aggressive gods was believed to be instant, such as the victim or someone in their close family being struck by lightning, snake bite, accident, heart attack or stroke. The more subtle deities on the other hand, preferred to take their time, so it could be months or years before the perpetrator was brought to justice. Meanwhile, the deity would ensure the warning signs were there for everyone to notice. This might manifest in the perpetrator suffering a chronic and debilitating illness, a stroke, or being prone to accidents or other misfortunes. The intent of this more subtle justice left the door open to the perpetrator of the crime to relent and own up to the truth of what they had done. But, victims lodging complaints with the deities must also ensure they take responsibility for their roles within the conflict, otherwise the complaint could backfire on them.

The anecdote was told of the very quick-tempered man who placed his bathing towel across his shoulder but then later, absent-mindedly looked desperately for the towel. Believing someone had stolen his towel and being the quick-tempered person he was, the man, in his haste, invoked the thunder god to use a streak of lightening to strike the perpetrator. Luckily, those around pointed out his folly before the god could act. Although his life was saved, the quick-tempered man had to pay several goats, quantities of alcohol and money at the thunder shrine for senselessly disturbing the busy god. The point of the story was to illustrate the intricate checks and balances traditionally guiding how humans invoked the spirit world, in their efforts to bring out the truth and satisfactorily mediate conflict.

The third and final domain of conflict mediation fell squarely within the sphere of the spirit world and involved accusations of witchcraft and sorcery. For these types of conflict, humans, no matter how endowed with *afemenunya*, or wisdom, were believed to be incapable of mediating adequately. Such conflicts were therefore best left to the spirit world to adjudicate. It was against this background that the issue bitterly divided the community and threatened to undermine cohesion. It all started when a Botoku man, recently retired from the military, collapsed and died unexpectedly in Accra, where he lived at the time. Because he was popular, relatively young and physically fit in the eyes of many people, and the death happened so suddenly and without warning, the whole Botoku community, both those living in the ancestral village and outside, were thrown into confusion. People were desperate to find answers.

The Botoku community in Accra met to plan for the corpse to be taken back to the village for burial. There was drinking, singing and wailing at the planning meeting and in the process, a man, a teacher by profession, at the time on study leave at Ghana's premier university at Legon and a close drinking friend of the deceased, apparently became possessed by the ghost of the deceased. Using his possessed friend as a conduit, the dead man provided a spiritual autopsy of his own death. He wanted everyone, especially his family and friends, to know that this death was not what destiny had given him from birth. Like many people, he too had dreams of achieving something big in life but in his experience, for every person trying to do something good, there were at least two people trying to bring him down.

He, as a boy, was lucky to have wonderful role models in his uncles who inspired him. One of them, a soldier, travelled all over the world to fight for the British in Burma during the big war. His bravery motivated him to join the Ghana army. Like his uncle before him, he too had to travel far away to fight on behalf of the OAU (Organization of African Unity) in the Congo defending the legitimate, but Soviet-backed, socialist government of Lumumba against the American-backed Mobutu's troops. In all his international peacekeeping roles in the army Botoku *Nuwo* (ancestors and deities) always ensured he returned unscarred. The same ancestors he believed helped him to survive not one, but three military coups in Ghana as a soldier. He was hoping to also do something important for Botoku in his retirement, as a way of showing his appreciation. But this was not to be. He was very angry and unable to find peace, because his death was not natural; he believed it was the work of witches who had cut his life short for no reason other than jealousy. The possessed medium then went on to name a woman back in the ancestral village as the leader of the gang of witches responsible for his death.

The incident was promptly reported to the chiefs and elders at Botoku. As custom demanded, the elders decided the case was beyond their human capacity to deal with effectively and hence the woman named had no choice but to go to *akagbe,* in order to clear her name. The *akagbe* ritual differed from place to place among Ewe people, but a common form was for the presiding spirit medium to give the accused herbal preparations to drink. If the person vomited, they were guilty and if not, it was a sign they were innocent. Punishment also differed from place to place, but typically ranged from the convicted person undergoing a ritual cleansing to neutralize the *adze* (witch) or *edzo* (sorcery), or being banished from the village. Punishment

93

might also extend to death, with the accused body burned in a wood fire after death, rather than being ceremoniously buried. If proven innocent, the person making the accusation would have to pay quantities of money, alcohol, sheep and goats, in order to pacify the accused. My sources' stories were full of gory details of how the concepts of *adze* (witchcraft) and *edzo* (sorcery) actually worked in practice, just to bring home the seriousness of the dilemma confronting the Botoku decision-makers and opinion leaders at the time.

Men and women could both be considered witches but the practice was more common with women; though the few males who became witches turned out to be some of the most notorious and destructive. Men were more likely to be accused of *edzo* or sorcery, which often involved the practitioner causing harm symbolically to an object representing the target or intended victim of the sorcery. By symbolically modeling to the relevant spirits the harm that the practitioner wished happened to their victim, the spirits then took over by carrying out the harm, all mystically of course.

Sorcery was not considered an inherited trait. Rather, the prospective practitioner made a conscious decision to obtain secrets of the trade from more established practitioners. But *adze* or witchcraft, on the other hand, was hereditary, as in the case of a grandmother passing it on to their favourite granddaughter. The witchcraft spirit could also be obtained unknowingly by a person from friends or strangers through close physical contact, as for example, the common practice among women to plait others' hair and groom each other. Whether hereditary or not, a woman, unlike their male counterpart practitioner of *edzo* (sorcery), thus had no choice as to whether they became *adze* (witch) or not. Being a witch was both literally and metaphorically like having a wild, vivid, imaginative, even bizarre, dream or nightmare.

The witchcraft spirit was believed to leave the body of the practitioner during sleep, transform itself into a bird or other animal or creature, and join the gang to which she belonged, since they often worked in gangs. Gang members were said to take turns nominating their favourite offspring, nieces, nephews, or grandchildren as sacrificial offerings for the enjoyment of the fraternity. Once nominated, whether the victim lived at Botoku, Accra or overseas, gang members were able to track them down and feast on their blood and flesh. It was believed all this happened in a matter of a single night when, to the uninitiated observer, both the victim and perpetrator were soundly asleep in their respective locations. Following a successful overnight feast, the victim then became sick or involved in an accident and died.

The question everyone asked following the sudden death of the ex-service man was which Botoku person would be the next prey for the witches. The whole atmosphere was tense, full of rumour, fear mongering and mistrust, as names of potential victims were bandied around. For the chiefs and elders, the only way forward was for the 'truth' to come out through the *akagbe* ritual. The large majority of Botoku people either supported or did not actively oppose the accused going through the ritual, apparently because it was the custom that their forbearers had handed down from generation to generation. They were unable to imagine or contemplate any other alternative course of action for dealing with the conflict. A vocal minority, mainly male community opinion leaders and development elites, were utterly opposed to the woman undergoing the *akanyinyi* ritual. The latter believed the whole *akanyinyi* practice was crude and inhuman and that no one should be compelled to undergo such a ritual against their wishes in this day and age. Those opposed to the ritual asked the woman to refuse.

Perhaps more importantly, they also secured the services of a lawyer for the woman who then lodged a complaint at the magistrate court at the regional capital, Ho. After nearly two years of family and friends not speaking to each other, several trips by the chiefs and elders to the Ho magistrate court, where the case was routinely adjourned, and several mediation efforts by groups of development leaders, the chiefs and elders resolved not to compel people to undergo *akanyinyi*. Since this incident, no Botoku person has been made to undergo the ritual, which the chiefs and elders now believe to be a major achievement for the community in its search for development or better future.

When asked to reflect upon the main factors that helped bring about a successful resolution, as well as lessons to guide the future, my sources on both sides of the argument identified remarkably similar sets of factors or enablers of change. For some, the emergence of a vocal minority prepared to draw a line in the sand and to risk their reputations and positions in order to say 'no' to something they deeply believed was wrong was the necessary first step. This enabled the woman, noted for her 'courage' and 'determination' by her supporters, and perjoratively as 'thick skinned' and 'stubborn' by her detractors, to stand up to the power and authority of the chiefs and elders.

Witchcraft and sorcery, and the associated trials by ordeal, were things the British colonial authorities had tried unsuccessfully to outlaw earlier and the practice simply went underground. Because belief in witchcraft remained so ingrained in the Ghanaian psyche, even the modern judiciary regarded it largely as too hot to touch. Unable to make final determination on matters pertaining to the spirit world, most magistrates and judges resorted to adjournments until the litigants, often out of frustration, withdrew the case to settle out of court. The financial and other costs of the intermittent trips to the Ho magistrate courts simply became too much for the chiefs and elders to bear. This was particularly the case after key Botoku citizen financiers of development projects refused the chiefs and elders' persistent requests for the financial donations and levies they needed in order to defend court cases and presumably enforce their decisions.

Others reflected upon the roles of various opinion and development leaders in presenting alternative stories to the chiefs and elders, beyond witchcraft and sorcery. The ex-service man whose death triggered the conflict in the first place, it was pointed out, drank alcohol and smoked cigarettes and hence was at a very high risk of heart and other circulatory diseases and illness. Furthermore, evidence from other villages was provided to show how improved access to facilities such as clean water led to reductions in infant mortality and morbidity, and hence witchcraft accusations, prompting leaders of those villages to wonder where the witches had gone. A final important enabling factor was the capacity of the mediators to come up with a compromise they believed was acceptable to all parties. Thus, the issue was not whether people believed in witchcraft or not. Rather, the question was whether it was appropriate for the chiefs and elders to compel a person, against her wish, to undergo a ritual that conflicted with her Christian faith. If the chiefs and elders really believed in the power of Botoku ancestors, deities and other spirits, then all they needed to do in cases such as the witchcraft case, was to pour libation (prayer) to the relevant spirits in the hope that such spirits would act in their own time.

Consequently, the argument continued, it was wrong for herbal concoctions prepared by humans, even if they were spirit mediums, to be used as the main tool for determining the truth in a conflict that squarely lay within the domain of the spirit world. One of the chiefs reflected during the course of this research: you cannot tell people what they should or should not believe in. As elders, however, they decided the best thing was to defer things that belonged to the spirit world solely to the spirits who should deal with it in their own time without any interference from humans.

Today, belief in witchcraft among the Botoku people, as in most parts of Ghana, remains as strong as ever. Mysticism, fear, mistrust and stress resulting from the threat of witchcraft abound. In fact, the fear of witchcraft, sorcery and other malevolent spirits largely explains the growing popularity of evangelical churches in present day Ghana, as worshippers flock in the hundreds and thousands seeking protection. In the context of the entrenched religiosity and mysticism, incremental changes to age-old customs and traditions, such as the decision by the Botoku people to outlaw the *akagbe* ritual, without necessarily challenging the belief in witchcraft itself, constitutes a significant outcome.

I have shown, through the range of case studies discussed in this chapter, attempts by the Botoku people to grapple with and find creative ways to adapt and reform age-old customs and traditions once regarded as unchangeable, as people's material circumstances, values and world views evolve. Clearly, a major part of any meaningful effort to promote development among traditionally oriented societies experiencing rapid change, such as Ghana and other developing countries, ought to focus on creating safe spaces for respectful but critical public deliberation or conversations among communities of people with regards to the extent to which their customs and traditions promote or undermine their search for a better future. In this context, we can then look at what can be done to improve the situation.

School cultural dance

97

Tsiami (spokesperson) pouring libation

Women singing funeral dirge

Chapter 8

Making a Living through Economic Participation

An important and obvious dimension of development is the ability to make a living through meaningful participation in economic activity. As noted throughout this book, the availability of apparently abundant land to grow crops and hunt for food was one reason the migrating ancestors elected to make their permanent home at Botoku in the first place. From the outset, the early settlers took advantage of the Volta River trade to participate in a variety of exchange activities. The opportunity to make a living was also one of the main reasons the Botoku people embraced, often enthusiastically, a wide range of new ideas under colonial rule such as schools; trade skills like carpentry and bricklaying; as well as cash-cropping, even though the latter was largely unsuccessful. The flooding of Botoku lands following the construction of the hydroelectric dam, combined with population growth, exerted pressures on arable lands, with the result that education, trade apprenticeships and small scale agribusiness came to be regarded as the main avenues towards economic participation for young people. Today, the main sources of income and sustenance for residents are subsistence farming and fishing, and raising animals. Through these, they are able to feed the family and to sell any excess for monetary income. There are also revenues from table top or small scale retail trade and street side cooking. Remittances from non-residents to families in the village are another major source of sustenance, especially for the elderly and infirm.

The Zambian economist, Dambisa Moyo (2009), pointed out how international aid, no matter how well intended, often had the perverse or negative impact of clouding out financial and social capital as well as breeding rampant corruption across Africa. What is less well-known is how even in the absence of blatant corruption, the notion of aid can seriously undermine motivation and resourcefulness at micro community level. In this chapter, I examine recent attempts, largely by non-residents, to use international NGO and other development aid income generation concepts and resources, as opportunities to promote economic participation within the village, and the difficulties and lessons arising. I decided to focus on income generation schemes resourced by international development aid because, as a sector, its share or contribution to the total economic output of the village, at least in the Botoku context, was absolutely non-existent or at best miniscule. Yet, the whole issue of development aid loomed disproportionally large in terms of people's hopes and expectations for fostering opportunities for economic participation, not only at Botoku but indeed across the entire African continent. Perhaps even more importantly, I wish to show how the very idea of aid or free money from rich countries, manna from heaven as some sincerely believed, if not handled strategically, not only creates community conflict and division, but also promotes dependency, undermining individual enterprise and drive; both of which are critical to economic development.

The single most significant attempt by the Botoku people to use development aid sources as an opportunity to improve incomes for local residents was an ambitious, if not particularly well thought through, five-year plan aimed at creating employment, as well as modernizing the village. Begun in the latter half of the 1980s by two well-meaning Botoku men living in Accra, the initiative dabbled in a wide variety of income generating activities, driven opportunistically by development aid funding. Rather than launching into how this experiment came about and the reasons it did or did not succeed, I wish to provide some background. Specifically, I feel it important to explain the unique nature of social stratification and inequalities within family units and clan groups in transitional societies, such as Ghana, experiencing rapid social change on the one hand, and the cultural interdependency of family and clan groups on the other. The main point I wish to make is the unique ways in which socio-economic inequality manifests within family units in transitional societies such as Ghana. This makes it hard, ethically and culturally, for the middle classes, or people with means, to ignore poverty, hence the strong desire, as the case studies will reveal, among many citizens to contribute, in whichever ways they can, towards greater economic participation for local residents.

I will draw upon two of my sources' stories to illustrate the point. These tales frequently used personal family circumstances to show inequality was not just something occurring across social class, as was often suggested by development literature. Perhaps even more important was how inequality manifests within family units, hence making it, in this particular context, much more real, and in your face, so to speak. For instance, in one family, the eldest of three sisters in their 50s and 60s born prior to Ghana becoming independent, had only two years of schooling; married before 20; had seven children, two of whom died. The husband also passed away leaving her with five children to support through subsistence farming and table top trade. Only two of her children made it through to high school. The second sister completed ten years of basic compulsory education implemented after Ghana became independent; worked as an administrative assistant in a government office; had two children, both of them educated - one to university level. The youngest of the three sisters went as far as teachers' college and became a school teacher; had three children, all of whom completed university.

In another family of five brothers in their 40s and 50s, one was under-employed in a very low paying role as an office cleaner; one was a subsistence farmer; and the other three were highly qualified professionals. In a third, younger family of four brothers in their 30s, one is a professionally qualified civil servant; one a tradesman; one a subsistence farmer; and the last one under-employed in what some feared were fraudulent activities, including possibly violent crimes. The point to be made is that in transitional societies, such as Ghana, it was individual members of a nuclear family, rather than whole family units, who belonged to different social classes. This contrasts sharply with developed countries where, except perhaps in the case of minority populations such as Aboriginal Australians, whole families, rather than individual members, often belonged to different social classes. In fact, in most western societies, the mainstream middle classes interact with vulnerable population sub-groups mainly in their professional roles as health care providers, case managers, doctors, teachers, social workers and legal aid lawyers. In the case of Ghana and similar societies, that is less likely the case. For those doing well, it was often their brother, sister, cousin, niece or nephew, rather than their patient or client, struggling to make ends meet.

Another story might explain how this unique social structure was made even more complex by the culturally interdependent nature of the relationships and obligations across extended family and clan groups, especially with regards to funerals and other rituals. This again made it harder for people with means, whether monetary or knowledge based, to ignore the plight of the less fortunate. For the Botoku people, my sources believe, there are four significant individuals central to a person's funeral rituals, once the chiefs and elders established there were no suspicious circumstances surrounding the death. The individuals playing these roles may change over time, but the roles themselves remain constant. First, there is *Vito* (literally father of the child) and *Vino* (mother of the child). These are not the deceased's biological father and mother. *Vito* comes from the uncles and great uncles of the father's side of the extended family, while *Vino* is the

101

aunties and great aunties of the mother's side. The roles are based on genealogy, rather than age, so a younger person can play *Vito* or *Vino*, even for an elderly person thrice their own age. The roles and responsibilities are many but for the purposes of this discussion it is these two people who, by custom, are responsible for the overall conduct of a person's funeral.

Children, spouses and other close family members and friends do have important roles and decisions in the process, but in terms of overall responsibility to ensure rituals are done properly, it is the *Vito* and *Vino* who take precedent. In times of grief, immediate family members are believed to be too emotionally affected so it is thought best to leave such matters in the hands of people a little bit removed and hence, presumably, able to make more rational decisions. The other two significant people are *Tovinyonu* (meaning the dead person's sister from the father's side) and *Tovintsu* (a brother from the father's side). But again, these two individuals are not the dead person's siblings but instead first, second, third and so forth cousins, from the father's side of the extended family. Traditionally, as soon as a person passed away the *Tovinyonu* and *Tovintsu* put their lives on hold, could not talk to people unless it was close family, should not eat certain types of food and would not shake hands with people. Until the deceased's properties are handed over to the legitimate next of kin, these two are the only people allowed to touch any personal belongings, including clothes to dress up the corpse. They also act, during the course of the funeral, as the conduits between the ancestors and the rest of the grieving family. An example might be when they apparently became possessed to reveal the causes of the death and the wishes of the dead person with regards to any unfinished business.

Despite education and Christian faith the twin roles of *Vito-Vino* and *Tovintsu-Tovinyonu* remain central to funeral rituals in Botoku, even if many aspects have become largely symbolic. Part of the reason people still value these institutions is because they provide frameworks for teaching young people, especially those living outside the village, about how families are connected. The point to be taken is that, no matter peoples' social status and place of residence, the relationships across extended families remains highly interdependent, making it harder for those better off to ignore those struggling to make ends meet. As one research participant succinctly put it, you just can't tell who is going to play *Tovi* for you when you pass on, meaning, no matter how poor a person, they may still be the most appropriate person to play *Tovi,* even for the richest.

For a minority of Botoku people, like in many parts of Ghana, the pressure on family and clan groups to look after each other can become too much to handle and they simply disconnect physically and emotionally, preferring to focus on the needs of their immediate family, though the broader ethical and cultural obligations invariably drag them back from time to time. The larger majority though find it too hard to sit back and do nothing. Some may take a sibling or cousin's child and put them through school or an apprenticeship, though such arrangements can sometimes result in exploitation when the person treats such children differently than their own biological children. Others may provide small amounts of capital to families back home to trade, as supplements to subsistence agriculture. Yet others, especially those in public office, would do whatever they could to find jobs or educational opportunities for families and friends, even though this might involve corrupt and unethical practices. Many believe this was a contributory factor to corruption in present day Ghana and other African countries.

It was against this perennial desire by those with the necessary means to help improve opportunities for others worse off, that the ambitious income generation initiative was launched in the latter half of the 1980s. The *tsiami,* or spokesperson, for one of my research groups explained. The original name of the project was Botoku Youth Association (BOYA) but the chiefs and elders later changed the name to Botoku Famers Association (BOFA). One of the two young men who began the organization in Accra was a professional adult educator. He was very experienced in dealing with NGOs and aid agencies. The first thing he did was write stories that were published in national and local newspapers announcing the formation of BOYA. The articles explained the goal of the organization was to improve employment and education opportunities in Botoku. The new organization also aimed to modernize the entire Botoku village to make it more attractive for young people to stay and make a living. The article went on to say initiatives such as BOYA were urgently needed throughout Ghana, in order to prevent thousands of school graduates heading towards cities and towns each year for jobs that did not exist. It was unethical and unacceptable for community leaders, church leaders, politicians and international aid agencies to continue to turn blind eyes to the increasing armies of under-employed youth throughout the country.

Readers were reminded of the negative consequences already resulting from young people lacking the opportunity to do anything meaningful with their lives. Some simply day dreamed in half depressed mental states, while others became involved in anti-social behaviours and activities such as prostitution and pick pocketing, the latter inevitably leading to more violent crime. Yet others would do anything, including crossing the treacherous Sahara desert, to get to Europe and other developed countries as economic refugees. Their aim was to seek jobs that many believed citizens of rich countries were no longer happy to undertake. The author believed this state of affairs undermined community values and norms about acceptable and unacceptable behaviour and that it was responsible for the rapid spread of HIV/AIDS as well as alcohol, marijuana and other drug abuse in Ghana. Reminding readers of the Ewe saying *afenya mewua ame o,* meaning a person's ancestral home will never fail them, the author invited 40 interested Botoku people (20 women and 20 men) to come forward with their names to join the organization. Each of the newspaper stories concluded by appealing to all international development agencies in the country, government organizations and other well wishers, to help the new initiative through financial donations; low interest loans; technical and materials support. The piece further added that if the initiative proved successful, it could serve as a model for other rural communities throughout Ghana.

Next the men wrote funding applications to as many development agencies as possible, informing them of the new organization and requesting financial and other support. Attached to each funding application were the newspaper publicity clippings. With the preparatory work in Accra behind them the project originators headed to the ancestral village where they informed the chiefs and elders of their plans. Included in the five-year plan were cooperative farms; cottage industries; a health centre; a *fiasa* or palace; a vocational school; village beautification such as tree planting; plans to tar the 18-km dirt road and access to low interest loans. Many at the meeting apparently thought the proposals looked too good to be true, but were nevertheless happy to support the effort. A local committee of five from the meeting agreed to work with the two young men to further develop ideas.

No sooner had the men left to return for Accra than another group of Botoku residents, also from Accra, arrived to meet with the chiefs and the elders. As elders and prominent Botoku development project financiers, the latter delegation were unhappy the two young men had used the names of *Togbe Tamtia* (paramount chief) and his elders in all their publicity and funding applications without first informing them. They were concerned the chiefs and elders would be liable in the event the project originators failed to pay back any loans they obtained. At a subsequent meeting of all parties, including the district level government representative who had been informed of the controversy, the chiefs and elders reprimanded the two young men for starting the initiative without their knowledge. For this reason, the original Botoku Youth Association was abolished and instantly replaced by a new one, the Botoku Farmers Association (BOFA), presumably to focus the plan more specifically on agriculture.

A new committee of four was accordingly set up to help the same two young men run the new organization, which by then had a total of 18 registered members - ten men and eight women. Despite the apparent resolution, the initial bitterness surrounding the conflict left such a bad taste in many people's mouths that the organization never fully recovered. An initial plot of land acquired to start a maize farm had to be abandoned because the relatives of the family head who offered the land, kicked against the offer. A subsequent acquisition was fully supported by all members of the relevant clan group owning the land, but this alienated the other clan groups, who were unhappy the BOFA project was being associated too closely with that particular clan. Since there was no money from any quarters initially, members provided labour on a communal basis while a loan was raised from a rural cooperative bank to purchase equipment and seeds. Meanwhile, a UNICEF official, the first of some two dozen development agency delegates to zoom in and out of Botoku inspecting the BOFA projects over the next several years, visited without providing any financial aid; though the possibility of building a child care facility was discussed.

The first tangible support came from the Canadian International Development Agency (CIDA) which offered quantities of cement, corrugated iron roofing sheets, planks, nails, a corn mill, chicken feed, 2000birds, plus cash of 1 million Ghana cedis (100 US dollars), for a poultry farm. Two bundles of roofing sheets left over after erecting the structures for the poultry and the corn mill were sold. The money generated from the sale, combined with the cash from CIDA, enabled BOFA to purchase an old vehicle. This was presumably to meet its own transport needs and to raise income from passenger services on the 18-km dirt road, so the bank loans could be repaid without waiting for the birds to mature. The sale of the iron sheets was promptly reported to the Castle (the seat of government in Accra located at what was originally a massive Portuguese slave holding castle, but until 2000 served as the headquarters of successive governments both colonial and post independent), that BOFA had embezzled development aid materials.

The organization was apparently exonerated upon investigation by the district government representative, but BOFA's problems were far from over. The engine in the old vehicle purchased, to help BOFA pay off its debts, collapsed beyond repair about a week after taking delivery. Meanwhile, on average eight of the poultry died daily after they started laying eggs. This was reported to the district agricultural officer at Kpeve but there were no funds available to purchase the recommended drugs and so local herbs were used to treat the birds. A delegation of nine from an NGO known as Mobi Squad came from Accra to advise the birds be sold and the funds used for pineapple farming, which the government promoted at the time as part of its efforts to diversify agricultural exports beyond cocoa and coffee. But by then it was too late, because all the birds died within a short period.

The rest of the BOFA story then became a catalogue of one hastily developed initiative after the other, depending on whatever funding was forthcoming. Thus, the German 'ambassador' (read diplomatic official) gave an amount of 1 million cedis (100 US dollars) intended for goat rearing. A structure was erected and 20 goats were bought. A veterinary officer came to inoculate the animals, but all died shortly after receiving the injections. The 'ambassador' (official) was promptly informed about the incident and he came to see things for himself. Another NGO known as ADRA inspected BOFA's maize farm, was happy about the progress, and donated eighty (80) bags of wheat and rice in food aid to the members to encourage them to work harder. Unfortunately, non-members were unhappy the wheat and rice was shared among BOFA members alone and for this reason, as by now was the pattern, letters were again sent to government officials complaining BOFA was embezzling food aid meant for Botoku as a whole. Aid from the Netherlands' African Centre was used to rear rabbits and manufacture soap, but the rabbits also died because BOFA members had no knowledge of rearing rabbits. Other development agencies continued to show interest, but the most significant of them all was an attempt to establish a vocational school to enhance skills development locally. Although BOFA succeeded in getting cement and other building materials from several development aid sources and the Ministry of Education provided teachers for the school, the lack of support and mistrust on the parts of the chiefs, elders and the established development elites, meant the school collapsed with only four of the original 45 intake students graduating, bringing a sad end to BOFA.

Despite the difficulties then, BOFA leaders at the time of this research were rather proud of half a dozen certificates of awards and recognition the group accumulated. These included an award to BOFA women for the quality of their *gari* at a national agricultural trade fair in Accra; an award to BOFA'a popular *Bobobo* dance group for coming first in a district cultural dance competition at Kpandu; and a poultry farming certificate of recognition signed by the secretary of agriculture.

For many of the research participants, BOFA failed woefully because of a combination of factors that resonated powerfully with the usual culprits of poor governance, and technical and managerial failures widely documented in the development literature. Included in these were a generation gap between the youth and the elderly; a lack of project planning and implementation capacity within the BOFA leadership, especially with regards risk assessment and management; as well as opportunistic and uncoordinated funding streams resulting from a silo mentality among aid agencies. While not disputing any of these as legitimate, others believed BOFA's problems were much deeper, and indeed were generally symptomatic of a larger problem. The issue was seen as symptomatic of a perennial failure, by both international development agencies and local project originators, to differentiate between aspects of economic participation that can appropriately be owned and managed communally, and aspects best left to individual enterprise and self-interest. The point to be taken is the BOFA story, though by any standards was the most unbelievably surreal, is far from unique.

The only other known instances in the history of Botoku when international development aid sources were used for income generation activities, similarly resulted in bitter community conflicts and disputes over how best to reward individual efforts. The story was told of a man, not from Botoku originally, but married and settled there in the 1960s and 70s. He had previously lived in Accra where he was exposed to the activities of the international NGOs and other development agencies that proliferated at the time. My sources remembered him as charismatic, charming and bigger than life; an orator and comedian with a loud infectious laugh able to maintain the attention of his audience for hours.

One day this man decided he could no longer live with his conscience, seeing many talented middle school graduates drift around the village because there were no opportunities for them to go on to high school. There had been largely fee-free education in Ghana since independence, but rural students, such as those from Botoku, still had to pay for their own boarding and lodging at high schools located mainly in the cities and towns. The cost of this, for agrarian populations, could be considerable. This meant many talented and motivated students simply could not proceed beyond the basic compulsory middle school education. So, what did he do? Each year as soon as the Common Entrance Examination results (the highly competitive national high school entry examinations at the time) were published, he collected the half a dozen or so top students from the village, not able to secure high school scholarships, into an Accra-bound mini bus. He would announce to the onlookers, in his characteristic dark humour that he was going to Accra to play on the good nature of his poor white friends.

For several days this man would take his young entourage of potential high school students from one western embassy and development aid agency to another, pleading to see the education attaché and other relevant officials. His dramatic and apparently contrived sad demeanor at each diplomatic mission or aid agency was the same. At each meeting he would break down in tears, crying and sobbing uncontrollably, as he announced each of the young people were orphaned, very bright and highly motivated, all while handing copies of their examination results to the officials to peruse. Although he was not always successful, he managed, over a three-year period, to secure financial support for at least seven students, enabling them to access a high school education. The entire community was most appreciative of his efforts.

When the same popular man, with financial support from international development aid sources, mobilized groups of young people to grow yams on a cooperative basis for sale, the initiative collapsed after only one planting season. Non-members of the cooperative were unhappy that, presumably, the name of Botoku as a whole was used to obtain development aid for the sole benefit of members of the cooperative. Within the cooperative there was also disquiet that some members did as little as possible, but expected to take as much as possible from the collective effort.

The story was also told of a piggery cooperative, initiated by a prominent politician from Botoku in 2004, with the aim of improving the earning capacity of women. A woman herself, she was acutely aware of the plight of rural women in particular and was committed to doing whatever she could to enable them to improve their situation. She initiated several successful projects, including a post office and market, which was also used as a venue for community meetings, and was working hard towards coal tarring of the

108

18-km dirt road. She was honoured by the chiefs and elders, and the entire Botoku community, for her contributions. As with the other income generation projects discussed however, the 25-member piggery cooperative was characterized from the outset by conflicts and disputes over people allegedly putting in as little as possible, yet expecting as much gain as possible. The result was that many of the members left disillusioned, while the project originator and others had to spend a great deal of time mediating between feuding factions within the cooperative at a time the organization was also said to be falling deeper and deeper into debt.

Finally, a young man from a nearby village reflected on his own sad experience with the World Vision child sponsorship program. Although strictly speaking not an income generation initiative, I included the child sponsorship story here because of the insight it gives about the extent to which such initiatives can undermine motivation, self exertion and resourcefulness within the recipient communities. The young man was in his late 20s at the time of the research. He said a man from his village living in Accra successfully arranged child sponsorships for three children, including himself when they were in junior secondary school. The man asked the school to nominate six of the brightest children. He then took photos of them in order to prepare the sponsorship applications. But before the photos were taken, he said with laughter, they had to change from their ordinary school uniforms into the tattered clothing that they normally wore to the farm. This was to show that they were really poor or orphaned. Luckily, for him, three of the applications, including the one for him were successful. His own sponsor was a nice and kind German woman. The woman had no children and her husband also died. This meant she only had herself and her dog to look after. Every now and then the World Vision person came to the village to take photos of the three children together with their school reports to send to their sponsors who, in turn, sent letters and photos of their families. Looking back on the whole experience, he said it was strange each time the word spread around that World Vision was coming to collect their school reports, you saw almost every school child in their tattered farm clothes lined up waiting for their photos to be taken for sponsorship. Everybody, for some reason, he said, believed that once you get a White person, who were all believed to be rich, willing to sponsor one child in the family, half the problem of that whole family was solved. He sincerely believed that the sponsorship would be enough to continue to boarding school for senior secondary school away from the village, after which the sponsor would take him to Germany. Then of course he could also help his brothers and sister to follow. He said what saddened him most was the fact that prior to the child sponsorship episode, parents and extended families, despite being poor, were still able to mobilize their resources in order to send children like himself to senior secondary school. As a result of all the expectations surrounding child sponsorship at the time, he believed, an entire cohort of children, himself included missed out on going to boarding school, because everybody was waiting for more and bigger sponsorships which never came.

Clearly, the main problem with all of these income generation experiments was not that the leadership was corrupt or lacked management skills; nor were they bad ideas. Most of the small scale commercial ventures, such as the piggery, poultry, passenger car services, corn mill, yam and maize farming, that apparently proved unwieldy and unmanageable for the cooperatives, were in many cases run reasonably successfully in the village by people with similar backgrounds through individual enterprise. Rather, the main problem was the failure to ground the projects in the locally relevant cultural norms and frameworks guiding cooperative efforts.

Like many Ghanaians, and indeed West Africans, Botoku people have always used cooperative labour as the basis for their material, social and spiritual protection. There was, however, a need to distinguish between different domains or types of cooperative efforts. The first, as already noted in previous chapters, was the public domain for projects such as road building and schools requiring all able-persons to participate. The other, and for the purposes of this discussion the most relevant, was the private domain. Known as *asikpli* (Ewe) or *susu* (Akan), this type of cooperative effort often involved groups of people with common interests and aspirations who, on the basis of trust and reputation, came together for the benefits of their members.

Take subsistence farming as an example. There were limited windows of opportunity for a farmer to slash and burn the field in preparation for planting. The planting itself needed to be carefully timed to coincide with the rains. Harvesting and storage needed to be done within the shortest possible time before pests and the weather exerted their toll. Instead of an individual and their family undertaking all these tasks day-in day-out on their own in relative isolation, half a dozen men or women might decide to combine their efforts, by taking turns working on each other's farms on a rotational basis.

Traditional forms of savings are another common example. A group of perhaps five self-employed traders or wage earners may decide to make fixed financial contributions of $5 dollars per month, amounting to a total of $25 every month. The individual contributors then take turns, at the end of each month, collecting the $25. The money was to be used for such things as capital to expand trade, purchasing capital goods, paying deposits on rental accommodations, or school fees for children.

Another locally relevant example my informants discussed was the local *akpetesi* (alcoholic spirit from fermented palm wine) distillery cooperatives. Banned by the colonial authorities in response to complaints by British traders that the locally produced gin competed with their imports, production occurred clandestinely under dangerously unsafe conditions. The newly independent government, under Kwame Nkrumah, legalized *akpeteshi* and other local spirits production from the 60s on, by encouraging distillers to form cooperatives as part of the broader socialist-inspired development agenda at the time. In this instance, the infrastructure for distilling the alcohol was owned by the cooperative as a whole, but each individual member was responsible for their own distilling, paying fixed amounts for each quantity of alcohol produced towards maintenance.

Whether piggery, poultry, *gari* making, goat rearing or yam farming, the locally viable and expedient arrangement would have been for the major capital infrastructure burdens, such as equipment, machinery, buildings, affordable credit, and economy of scale in marketing, that individuals could not normally afford on their own accord, to be collectively owned to create the necessary opportunities for those interested to take advantage. But, the actual responsibility for exerting oneself in response to available opportunities to produce or create value must be left to individual self-interest and motivation. Those interested then contributed mutually agreed upon percentages of their total output or value generated, towards renewing and sustaining the communally-owned infrastructure. This way, opportunities for economic participation can be promoted, but not at the expense of individual motivation and enterprise, as appeared to be the case with all the income generation initiatives so far discussed.

The last two projects identified as relevant to economic participation in the recent history of the village, happened to be those I initiated as part of my ongoing community development contributions, following my migration to Australia. Begun in 2000, the first initiative was an education trust designed to improve school outcomes for local Botoku students from pre-school through to the junior secondary school (JSS), which had, since the late 80s, replaced middle schools. The other project aimed to provide access to low interest credit, mainly to women engaged in small scale enterprises. One of the things participants said they found most valuable about my research project was the opportunity it offered them to share and listen to each other's stories and experiences. Irrespective of socio-economic status or place of residence, everyone grappled with the cultural expectations that families would look after each other, on the one hand, and the ever growing inequalities between members on the other. I was struck that a significant proportion of the diaspora research participants and their families and friends, both African and not, expressed a strong desire to do something to help their ancestral communities back in Africa, but either did not know where to start, or were too scared to risk their scarce resources given the endemic corruption and mismanagement.

It was against this background that I decided to include the two projects initiated by me, simply to illustrate some of the ways I have dealt, at a personal level, with these challenges. Before examining the two projects it is necessary for me to briefly outline my personal ethics, developed over the years, that guides my own approach to helping others, in order to put the two projects in context. Like any Ghanaian, and for that matter African in my situation, being one of the first to access higher education in my family, necessarily created huge income gaps between others and myself. The first step, I found empowering in my attempts to grapple with the cultural expectation that whatever belonged to one person in the family belonged to the whole family, was accepting the ethical and cultural responsibility from an early age. I understood it was desirable and even noble to use a proportion of my income for the benefit of others, whether family or not. Next, I decided that 'needs' rather than 'wants' would, as much as possible, guide my own patterns of consumption in life, for the simple and obvious reason that as humans our wants are so unlimited and insatiable. There is a distinct difference between what we want and actually need, materially or otherwise, to live fulfilled and flourishing lives. Having taken these foundational steps I was then confronted with perhaps an even bigger dilemma. What was the most ethical way of rationing the relatively limited resources at my disposal in relation to the ever-increasing, often urgent, needs surrounding me? In other words, no matter how hefty the salary packet, I was still only one individual in the midst of countless relevant people in desperate need. It was simply not possible for me to meet everyone's needs.

A turning point for me came when I decided that, like any initiative in life, I needed to set my own ground rules to guide how I supported others and, where possible, to make these rules known to those affected. First, except for the frail, aged and other disabled, I decided not to give money to people generally to satisfy immediate consumption needs, no matter how essential. Second, and this is particularly relevant to this discussion, I treated any support to people as an investment with the expectation that it would yield returns, not necessarily in narrowly defined profit terms, but rather a return that enhanced the capacity of the beneficiary to become more self-reliant. A third element of the ground rules was that, as Ewe people say, a person must be willing to lift their own load to knee level before others could help lift it from there onto the head. In other words, in a situation where the needs are so huge and the available resources so limited, I cannot afford to help everyone in need to start doing something from scratch. The risks of failing are too high. I chose to value add to what people were already doing, instead of helping them start new things. So, if a person manages to send their child to school or trade apprenticeship training and halfway through the going becomes too difficult, through no fault of theirs, then I was happy to come to their aid. Or, if a person was already trading, then I was happy to assist them to expand or diversify. The idea here is to focus on people who show potential within the relevant target groups, with the hope that they too would be able to support at least themselves and possibly others. The ethics of right and wrong of this, essentially trickle down economic philosophy, can be debated ad nauseam, but for me and many of my research participants, such boundaries constitute one way of achieving clarity about what is possible and what is not. It helps me maintain my own sanity.

The final point in my ground rules was an acknowledgement that individual charity, though important, was only a small part of the solution to poverty in the midst of plenty. Hence, my lifetime intellectual and political interests in evidence-based government policies that enhance the capacity of individuals, family groups, and broader communities to achieve health and wellbeing. These include universally accessible quality formal education and primary health care, taxation, and other policy instruments to reduce social disparities or inequalities, while fostering personal motivation and enterprise (WHO Commission on Social Determinants of Health, 2008).

Against such a background of personal ethics of practice, the Botoku Education Trust was developed, in response to community concerns that the quality of formal education in Botoku had deteriorated drastically since the

1970s. Among the factors impacting this were significant erosion in real incomes and purchasing power and hence, the status and respect for teachers, especially in rural areas. Like most Ghanaian public sector employees, teachers' salaries were, and still are so low, they cannot support a single person, let alone a family. Urban teachers responded, largely, by putting in as little effort as possible to their formal day time jobs, preferring to reserve their energies for private, fee for service tutoring in the evenings and on weekends. No matter the cost, Ghanaians across the board willingly patronized these, because of the extremely competitive nature of the education environment. Since few rural dwellers could afford to pay private tutors, teachers in these areas either spent half their working time at school and half on market gardens and other activities to supplement their incomes, or simply became frustrated and cynical. The result is a vicious cycle; lack of teacher motivation leads to poor school outcomes, which, in turn, results in poor parental and student motivation.

Yet most Ghanaians, whether urban or rural, believe strongly that in today's world giving a child the best education possible is like giving that child the key to life with which to look for, chase after and negotiate opportunities, no matter where they may find themselves. In other words, for the Botoku people and indeed Ghanaians generally, mobility or travel in chase of opportunities is part of normal life, and the best families and communities can do for young people, is to give them the necessary knowledge, skills and value systems with which to hopefully "fit in", no matter where their desire to improve their lot in life may take them. Not surprisingly, throughout this research there was no sense of moral panic as one often finds within international development circles about the fact two-thirds of the Botoku citizens live outside the village. On the contrary, the main concern was how to ensure that people have the capacity to participate in meaningful social and economic activity, irrespective of where they live, so as to be of benefit not only to their families, but also to the Botoku ancestral community as a whole.

In focusing on education as a priority issue, I was obviously influenced by my own experience and research interest in the potential power of education in transforming human relationships and improving health and wellbeing. There are two broad ways of looking at the effects of education on health and wellbeing. One is that in modern society your level of knowledge and skills and the values you hold largely determine your earning capacity and status in society, and hence your health. Higher incomes make it possible for people to want and to afford better food, healthier living conditions and better health care. The other way of looking at the effect of education is the way intellectual training and nourishment for the brain dramatically enhanced people's capacity to take the initiative to achieve what analysts have called the difficult task of living wisely in increasingly complex modern societies.

Based on my own personal experience and years of thinking, researching and writing about the relationships between formal education and health, I came to the conclusion that education leads to knowledge (information), attitudes (values) and skills (techniques), a combination of which is central to one's ability to make healthy choices in modern life. The latter includes having fewer children, which is critically important in the context of working towards sustainable living in Africa. As a result, following conversations with the chiefs and elders and key Botoku educators, I decided to a set up the education trust as a mechanism for engaging and focusing the broader community, as well as the relevant policy makers, towards locally relevant solutions.

My first step was to lay down the ground rules. As founder and patron, I would contribute a fixed amount per annum to the trust, as long as I continued to work. The chairperson of the board of trustees would be appointed by me. The chairperson would have maximum autonomy in selecting trustees for the day to day management of the trust. Other key elements of these ground rules were: that administrative costs could not exceed ten per cent of income; the trust must raise funds to supplement my annual contributions; the trust must invest portions of their incomes to ensure sustainability beyond my resource commitments; I would periodically resource a person with some distance from the trust to monitor performance; and finally, the chairperson must report on the state of the trust to me annually. Families, friends and colleagues in Australia, New Zealand and Germany have also contributed to the trust from time to time.

The five-member board of trustees at the time of the research includes three professionally trained teachers, two people with experience in running their own small business and a lawyer. Since 2000, the trust has been involved in a range of activities, including bestowing awards to students for their academic and other leadership achievements; financial awards to teachers and community members for contributions to education; advocacy and lobbying for resources including qualified and motivated teachers; and general community awareness, engagement and celebration of education. Despite reported modest improvements, like most Ghanaian rural areas, the quality of formal education at Botoku remains poor, but the trust has become an integral and valued part of the community infrastructure, with consistently positive feedback about its contributions.

Of particular relevance to this discussion is the aspect of social enterprise; that is to say, using the principles of business enterprise to achieve the social objectives of the trust. Although funerals, festivals and community development fundraising events frequently attract large numbers of people to Botoku, the facilities required to logistically cater for these occasions was always a problem. The trust identified this as an investment opportunity and, within the first two years, purchased 120 plastic chairs and 60 sleeping mattresses for rental purposes. Although the rents charged were minimal, the returns to the trust, by rural Ghanaian standards, have been significant. At the time of writing this, the trust hoped to set aside enough savings to purchase quantities of canopies for rent as well. Besides yielding additional income, trustees believed canopies would be good for the environment, since they would eliminate the event-based need to cut down trees and palm fronds for shade, still the case with major events in many parts of rural Ghana.

The other project, a pilot initiative designed to improve access to low interest credit to local women, was essentially a formalization of something I have always done informally over the years. As noted earlier, for most Ghanaians and other Africans in my situation, it has been a common practice for those with means to offer credit to family and friends, to undertake a variety of ventures. Some of these loans may, or may never, be paid back. Partly because of a growing demand for such support in relation to the resources available at my disposal, and partly because of all the difficulties encountered by the income generation projects discussed earlier, I decided to pilot a scheme that provided opportunities for people to improve their economic participation, without undermining individual drive and motivation.

Despite the concept of micro finance, and more recently micro insurance, being popular and booming in Ghanaian cities and towns, rural people still lacked access to such facilities. With the help of two people with backgrounds in enterprise development (one of them a recently retired banker), groups of interested women were asked to organize themselves into a cooperative. In this case, with support from family and friends, I provided resources to open a savings account with a nearby rural bank to serve as surety, or collateral, for the women who, for the first time, were able to

116

access bank credit. Because the interest charged by the bank was too high in relation to the returns on their small enterprises, I also decided to subsidize the rates on behalf of the women, making it affordable for them. Of the 15 people who started, only two dropped out of the program after 2 years, and both for entirely understandable reasons. Although demand for the program remains high, cheaper alternative credit sources would need to be found before other groups could be supported sustainably.

Two main conclusions can be drawn from this chapter. The first one relates to the need to distinguish between different spheres or domains of economic activity and participation. Just as local cultural norms and expectations were central to citizen contribution towards community infrastructure projects, so too were reciprocal relationships between clan and family groups motivating factors behind non-resident commitment to promoting opportunities for economic participation back in the ancestral village. There is a need to clearly differentiate between aspects of economic participation able to be done or owned communally, and those that ought to rely predominantly on individual enterprise and responsibility. Failure to make this important distinction is one reason many income generation projects, no matter how well-intended, fail to achieve their objectives.

The other conclusion to draw, is that the failures and limitations of the various initiatives discussed in this chapter should not overshadow the real community strengths, as far as the potential to achieve economic participation is concerned. The emphasis on education and employment creation as key to lifting the rural poor out of poverty and misery is basically a sound aspiration. Equally sound is the degree of motivation and willingness of rural African communities, such as Botoku, to jump at any opportunity for meaningful economic participation, no matter where it comes from. What is becoming clear is that, in an increasingly globalized world, there are serious limitations to how much small communities like Botoku, or indeed whole countries like Ghana, can do to improve education and employment opportunities in the absence of global partnerships based on mutually beneficial schemes for poor and rich countries alike.

I will draw upon a 2010 seminal global workforce trends report, *Creating Jobs in a Global Economy,* published jointly by the international recruitment agency Hays and economic forecaster Oxford Economics, to illustrate the point. Just as Ghanaians and other Africans are risking their lives to cross the Sahara Desert in search of jobs that they believe people in rich countries no longer want to do, the report forecasts dramatic and unprecedented movements of workforce, power and wealth across the globe over the next 20 years. The world's working-age population is expected to increase by more than a billion people during this timeframe. However, all of this growth will be in developing economies. The developed world will see its workforce, by comparison, shrink and age. While everyone is talking about the growth in the Chinese population, the evidence suggests that China's working age population, sooner rather than later, will plateau or level-up and then decline. Yet according to the report, no one is talking about how industries will employ the extra billion people who will soon be looking for work in India, Africa and South America. This, the report challenges, can be a huge opportunity if governments and industries get it right, by removing barriers to labour mobility across national borders.

There exists an equally dramatic potential social problem for everyone, both poor and rich countries alike, if, as a global community, we get it wrong. Included in the report's five-point action plan are a need to keep national borders open for the movement of skilled labour between developed and developing countries in both directions; and agreement through forums such as the G20 on an international code to facilitate skilled employee migration to replace the current chaotic national and regional piecemeal approaches. Central to the strategy is greater investment in education and employment in developing countries for the estimated 1 billion potential workforce, as smart investment opportunities by themselves, and for the public good. As well as averting the potential for social dissatisfaction and unrest if such labour were left idle, lifting living standards for this 1 billion people through education is also the surest way to finally see the global population stabilized and possibly begin to decline across all regions of the world. In chapter 10, the last substantive chapter in this book, I return to some of these ideas as part of canvassing possible ways forward. Before doing this, however, I hope to show in the next chapter how, for the Botoku people, development was also about identity. It was about having a place to call home where, even if everything else failed, people could always return in old age, die and be buried, or simply connect with spiritually as needed.

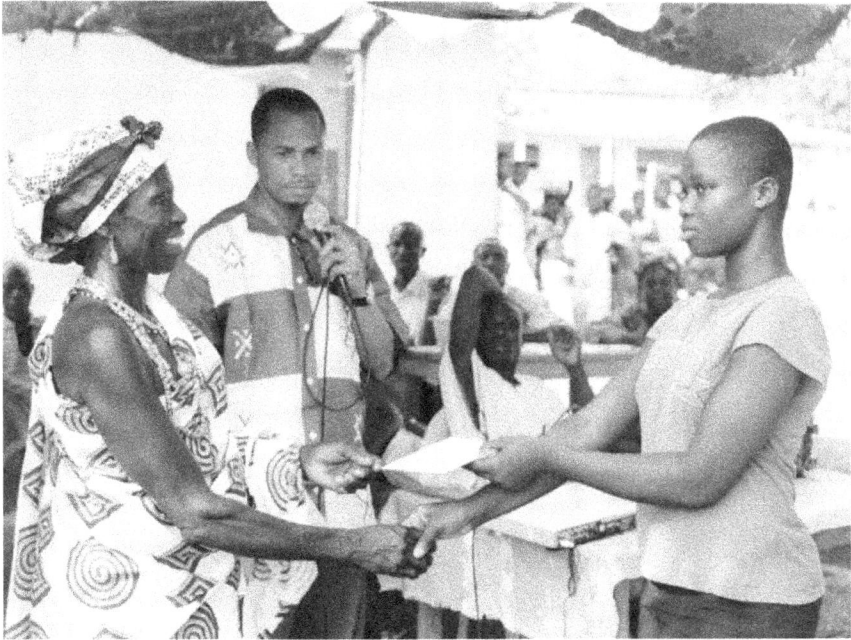

Female chief presenting education trust award to student

School cultural dance at education awards ceremony

Chapter 9

An Ancestral Home or Place to Connect

For the Botoku people, the quest for a better future through development was also about having an ancestral home, or a place to connect or relate. As already noted throughout this book, particularly in chapter 7, an ancestral land on which to be buried or have funeral rituals conducted was a major way the Botoku people, and indeed most Ghanaians, express connection to ancestral villages and towns. But there were a range of other ways through which connection was expressed. In a globalized world where people, like investment capital, are increasingly moving on large scales within and across national boundaries in search of better life, connection to a place, spiritual or otherwise, becomes an important cultural resource for strengthening identity, life purpose and belonging, irrespective of where people live. In this chapter, I draw upon my own experiences as participant observer, as well as informant narratives in order to highlight a range of other intricate ways in which connection to ancestral home might be expressed.

In Ghana, the long Easter weekend was a time most people returned to their ancestral villages and towns for fundraising events for the purposes of improving the living conditions there. For several weeks leading up to Easter, the newspapers, airwaves and more recently television stations, would be filled with largely urban-based rural development associations announcing forthcoming fundraising events and urging all citizens, including those living overseas, to return to the relevant ancestral homes to lend their support. In the weeks following Easter, the media would similarly be filled with reports of how much various villages and towns were able to raise, the projects being funded and information on future development aspirations. Probably the most spectacular of these annual events was the one organized by the Kwahu people in the eastern region of Ghana. Taking advantage of their serene and cooler mountainous climates, these weekend festivities were climaxed with breathtaking hang glides from the top of the escarpment to the bottom, and attracted hundreds of hang gliding enthusiasts from all over the world.

Against this background, I attended the 2010 Easter weekend development fundraising event at Botoku, as part of finalising the research for this book. I arrived in the village very late on Good Friday and so missed the activities of that day. At cockcrow the following dawn, the whole village was woken by the sound of a whistle calling all interested people to begin a 12km return walk to nearby Tsrukpe village to kick off the day's activities. Still suffering jet lag from the ten-hour time difference between Australia and Ghana, I was one of the last people to struggle out of bed to start the walk. At about 3kms, I caught up with the group. Soon after we met a group of school children who had jogged the entire distance and were already on their way home. The organizers reprimanded them for disobeying orders not to run and to stay part of the group. A decision was made that everyone was free to walk or jog at their own pace, but were asked to wait at the entrance to nearby villages so they could all sing and march through as a group; the main reason being to show respect to the other villages by passing through in an orderly fashion. A head count revealed 73 people, ranging from 12 years to the 70 something year olds, with the median age in the 30s, who walked the entire 12-km return trip. The actual number participating was much higher though, since some only went part of the way.

The early morning walk was rounded off by stretches on the soccer field, where the organizers reminded people, especially sedentary office workers, about the importance of daily physical activity. There were two football matches in the afternoon. Women residents in the village played their non-resident counterparts. This was followed by non-resident men playing resident men. In the evening there was a large bonfire, *bobobo* popular music with dancing, attended by an estimated 200 people of all ages, and lasting until midnight. Sunday was left open so people of faith could take part in the Easter church activities, though several development meetings were also held, including the Botoku Education Trust, which I attended. Monday was earmarked for the main fundraising and began at first light with a 10km return bicycle riding competition to the nearby Tsoxor village.

On my way back from the bicycle trip, I noticed the chiefs and elders had gathered in front of the paramount chief's *fiasa* (palace) in what appeared to be deep and serious deliberation. I gave up on the last half kilometre of the competition to join them; by that time all of the competitors except me had crossed the finish line anyway. Since the proceedings were already underway, those of us joining late had to wait patiently until towards the end when the *tsiami* or spokesperson explained what it was all about. Apparently several days previous, when all the last minute preparations (meetings, mobile phone calls and text messages) for the fundraising event were going on, a woman, believed to be possessed by the ancestral spirits, revealed that something terrible was likely to happen. She said unless the elders took steps to protect the village, the accidents would mar the whole fundraising activity. A two-person delegation was immediately dispatched to a nearby shrine to consult the ancestors for more information. According to the oracle, the ancestors and deities were unhappy and even angry, because many people were neglecting them due to Christianity. Young people were also said to be dabbling in sorcery, or the art of manipulating evil spirits for selfish purposes. All these were serious taboos for the ancestors and had to stop. If the fundraising were to proceed peacefully, the elders had to offer a large ram and a pot of palm wine to pacify the ancestors. Once the festivities were over, the elders should assemble the whole village and encourage them to recommit to looking after the ancestral spirits and deities, citing the case of the departed and well-respected former paramount chief, who was a committed Christian but also a most successful chief. In other words, people did not necessarily have to choose one or the other. The palm wine, which they had just shared, was part of the offerings.

An interesting aspect of the whole event was that, while the educated, mainly Christian, development leadership was busy organizing the practical logistics of the fundraising, the elders were in the background, totally unbeknownst to the development leaders, doing their own thing to ensure everything went well. With all their behind doors activities, the elders kept the entire gathering waiting at the durbar grounds for more than an hour, until they eventually arrived in their colourful clothes and ornaments for the fundraising event to formally start. The fundraising itself was deliberately organized to be fun, even if some of the techniques used were rather ironic.

Following the opening speeches, including an opportunity for me to narrate key findings from this research for community feedback, the MC handed the stage over to a non resident woman in her 30s with a background in community development and retail enterprise to appeal for funds. The first thing she did was to invite six prominent citizens, among them female and male chiefs, politicians and high ranking professionals, to step forward and take the empty seats in the middle of the gathering. She then asked the crowd if they would be willing to do whatever it took to save these six important people if something were to happen to, or threaten them. Applause from those gathered showed their consent. The problem, she went on, was that all six were now in *awuba* (chapter 4). Ironically, *awuba* was a form of domestic slavery, which until the 20th century, was common in most parts of Ghana. In this, a family or whole village, were prepared to pawn one of their own in times of need to secure a loan or favour. This then had to be repaid in order to redeem the person; a practice that became exploited by selling such pawns into permanent slavery for export. This meant Botoku was in a big trouble and had decided the only way out was to pawn these important people.

She called on all concerned citizens and their friends to come forward and donate generously, in order to redeem the six. The longer the six remained in *awuba,* the greater the shame for every Botoku person. She repeated this mantra over and over as the contributions came in for their redemption. This was followed by a competition between people born on each of the seven days of the week (southern Ghanaians normally name children according to the week day of their birth), as well as competition between men and women. Farm and other produce, donated mainly by residents, was then auctioned to the highest bidder, often to the non-resident visitors and invited guests. A total of three million cedis (nearly $3,000 US) was raised, in addition to other items including four computers, donated by a Botoku businessman to the schools. Although the case story raises several interesting issues for the purposes of this discussion, the main point to make is that, for some of the Botoku people, connection to ancestral home was an opportunity for both residents and non-residents to get together from time to time, to deliberate and, where possible, take action towards the physical, social and spiritual improvement of the village. But, for the large majority, the fundraising was also an opportunity to reconnect with family and friends, have fun, unwind from the stresses of urban living, speak in their own language and expose young people living outside the village to their cultural heritage.

Another way in which people expressed connection to the ancestral village was keeping a home where they hoped to retire in old age. For my sources, there are two types of retirement. There are those who, no matter their social status and income, consciously plan for retirement back in the village. This category they called 'good retirement.' Then there are those who, for a range of reasons, did not actively plan but rather, found 'retirement' back in the village thrust upon them because of a lack of options. This represented what they believed to be 'bad retirement.' In Ghana, few people can live on their wages and salaries, let alone pensions. Perhaps even more serious is the that fact that self-employed and under-employed people, who constitute a greater proportion of the work force, simply do not have any old age support, except that coming from families. This and other factors make the ancestral home a cheaper retirement option for many people, and

124

desirable except for barriers such as lack of services, financial demands from extended families and the fear that return to the village constituted failure. For some Botoku non-residents, especially those whose jobs are available in rural settings, such as teachers, a common strategy was to seek a job transfer closer to the village three to five years before retirement, so they could settle back in before formally retiring.

The story was frequently repeated of the couple who, as noted in chapter seven, approached the chiefs and elders on their retirement to allow them to bring their pet dog back to the village. This man left Botoku at a young age to go to boarding school in the 1950s. From there he obtained a former Soviet Union scholarship (one of the main planks in the ideological war to win the hearts and minds of the emergent developing country's political and intellectual leadership), where he spent seven years studying mining engineering in Russia. He returned to Ghana to take up an academic position at a university school of mines. He spoke Ewe, English, Russian, and other Ghanaian languages such as Akan and Buem, all fluently. His wife, also from Botoku, similarly left the village very early to go to boarding school, trained as a nurse and later settled with her husband, working as midwife until their retirement. Their children, all well-educated, worked in different parts of the country, including one in the UK. The couple, more so the woman, like other retirees who consciously planned their retirements, lived a very busy life back in the village. They maintained a large market garden full of vegetables and fruits, and kept goats, chicken and other animals for consumption. Besides this, the man, for a while, became the acting chief for his clan because the younger substantive chief still worked outside the village and returned home only from time to time. People valued this latter role because, like other retirees, his presence injected new, old blood, so to speak, into the community in the form of ideas and technical know-how. The woman on the other hand, when she was not working in the garden, ran a small chemical shop selling essential medicines. The most valuable aspect of her contribution, according to my sources, was as the *de facto* village doctor, providing free medical advice on anything from HIV/AIDS; pre and post natal care; high blood pressure; malaria; and most importantly, I discovered through a personal family experience, palliative care, something so needed in rural Ghanaian settings.

Asked why, after a life of relative material comfort, they decided to return to the village (at a time when electricity had not even yet arrived) their response, in unison, was *koklo tsitsi ekpo nu wo kuo de,* meaning an old and

125

tired chicken invariably returns to die in front of its coop. While the socio-economic status of this particular couple makes them atypical of many expressing connection through retirement back to the village, my sources narrated several other case stories to emphasize that active planning, rather than material means, was probably the most important factor in explaining whether a person had a bad or good retirement. Again, the main point here is that there are windows of opportunity for governments and social policy-makers to proactively assist interested urban dwellers in making smoother transitions back to their ancestral homes, should they so decide. As well as injecting new capacities into rural communities in the form of ideas, technical knowledge and other expertise, such investments could also ease pressures on urban facilities.

The ancestral home was also, for some, a sanctuary to which families turned no matter where they lived, in times of disease, illness and misfortune, especially mental illness and other psychosocial problems. Mental illness is devastating, not only for the sufferer and the family, but also for the wider community. In a community where almost everyone is related to each other, there is hardly anyone not in some way affected by the advent of mental illness. To most people, the sudden appearance of mental illness in the family can even kill close family members out of shock or worry. This was widely believed to be the case when a mother caring for a daughter suffering from mental illness at the start of this study, was said to have literally 'dropped dead' when she was informed her son had developed a similar illness. A father was suddenly taken ill and later died at hospital, apparently after seeing the condition of his son at a psychiatric hospital. What is more, the appearance of mental illness also creates suspicion and tension among people closely associated with the sufferer, because of the possibility of someone from the group being accused of being spiritually responsible for the problem. Mental illness therefore poses a real threat to family and community cohesion.

Unfortunately, mental illness is also an area the modern Ghanaian health care system is particularly poorly equipped to address. Although there is a clinic with a midwife and a community nurse at Botoku, neither of them, at the time of this study, was trained to deal with mental health issues. On the flip side, Botoku, like most rural Ghanaian villages and towns, was well endowed with a range of spiritual healers who catered to people suffering from mental illnesses and also palliative or end of life conditions.

In the context of the pressures and stresses of life associated with rapid and pervasive social change in Ghana, the ancestral village, despite material poverty and lack of modern services and facilities, appeared on the surface to continue to provide better protection against mental illness, vis-à-vis alien urban settings, though the exact mechanisms required further research. Out of the 14 people my sources identified as experiencing different forms and severities of mental illness in the village at the time of this study, for example, nine of them, or 64%, developed their illnesses outside the village, often in urban settings, before they were taken back to the ancestral home for care. For better or worse, the evidence suggests that spiritual healers, and indeed the familiarity of the ancestral villages and towns, will continue to play major roles in caring for people experiencing mental illness and other disabilities for a very long time to come. Clearly, policies are required to strengthen the capacity of rural communities and family caregivers, not only to better support those experiencing mental illness, but also for these people to look after their own health and well-being.

At the other end of the spectrum of physical connectedness to the ancestral home are people's mental, emotional and spiritual connections. Although those whose connection was primarily physical also expressed a range of other mental and spiritual dimensions of connection, my interest here lies mainly in the international diaspora who, for obvious reasons, happened to be the most physically separated. The following personal story, narrated by one of my research participants, provided some insight into how the international diaspora, especially the second and third generations, seek to deal with the Ghanaian, and indeed African heritage, even in the absence of any obvious opportunities or a need to connect physically.

A tertiary student in her early 20s told the story of her grandfather. He was apparently among the first groups of students supported on scholarships by the newly independent Ghanaian government in the 1950s, to study in the UK as part of the capacity development agenda destined to build the new nation. While there, he met and befriended her grandmother, a local girl on the same street in a small university town. Her father was the result of the brief union, which ended when her grandfather returned home after his studies as stipulated by the scholarship. Because of the racism of the time, her grandmother had to move to a bigger city, where things were a little more anonymous, to bring up her child. He grew up, met and married the girl's mother, also an English woman. This, according to my source, makes her a quarter, third-generation Ghanaian; and for that matter African. Her own

127

father had never been to Ghana, although he talked about it from time to time when she was a child. She herself was brought up in every way British. Since her father introduced her to soccer as a child she had always had her favourite soccer club, which she would do anything to support. Growing up she felt, every now and then, that there was something missing, especially when the word 'Africa' came up in conversation, but she didn't really pay much attention to it. Looking back, fitting in with her peers was the most important thing.

This was her life, until one day it all unraveled in front of her. Whether in the church, in the pub to have a beer, which as a good English woman she said she enjoyed, or at soccer matches with her friends, the new people she met always had some way of reminding her she was different. While most of these were what she described as benign curiosity, she said, every now and then, it hit her that she was being judged on the basis of her heritage. As a result she started asking the basic existential questions of herself. What is my story and who am I? She said the more she became aware of and accepted her African heritage, in her own words, as only one piece in a complex jigsaw puzzle, the happier she became as a person. While she may or may not visit her African roots one day, she welcomed this sort of reflective (research) conversation, which she hoped not to deny her own children one day, as had been her experience growing up. This case story, which in many ways resonated with several second and third generation diaspora interviewed for this research, suggests that, for those physically separated through distance or otherwise, connection to ancestral roots may simply involve the capacity to accept the different or relevant elements in a person's identity or background.

In this chapter, I have illustrated some other ways in which the Botoku people and indeed other Ghanaians, no matter where they lived, expressed connection to their ancestral homes. For some non-residents, no matter how long they had been away from the ancestral village, it remained the place where their hearts always belonged. It was therefore in their interests to ensure Botoku remained functional, and hopefully even a thriving second home, to provide shelter from the trappings of urban life. It was a place to seek sanctuary in times of illness and other misfortunes. It was also a place to spend retirement years and eventually to die and be buried. Yet, for others, wherever they had settled and made a living was a home for them. The latter did not realistically see themselves, or their children's children, ever returning to Botoku on any long-term basis or expressing their connection in a physical sense. Connection for them was essentially knowledge of an ancestral home they could pass on to curious and interested children and grandchildren. The point to make is the role that connection to ancestral place can play in promoting a sense of belonging, identity and wellbeing in an increasingly globalised world. This provides opportunities for designing development policies that transcend the conventional urban versus rural dichotomy, and hopefully promote thriving rural communities, at the same time easing pressures on overloaded urban services and facilities.

In the final substantive chapter I hope to bring together the key findings from the various chapters in order to develop an integrated model of development.

Women having fun and games at development weekend

Author narrating stories from the book at the development forum

Female chiefs walk to Durbar grounds

Female footballers as part of development weekend

Fun walk as part of development fund raising weekend

Male chiefs on their way to development forum

Women fun game

Chapter 10

An Integrated Model of Development

The purpose of this chapter, the last substantive, is to bring together the various findings of the oral history research as a whole, as presented in the different chapters of the book, into a single theoretical model of development.

Theoretical models and frameworks can be tools to help people simplify and make sense of such complex and difficult to articulate social realities as development, or the quest for a better future. After presenting the theoretical model of development, as experienced and narrated by the Botoku people, I tried briefly to locate or ground this micro community perspective within the broader Ghanaian, and indeed international development trends. The aim was to determine the extent to which this local small scale Botoku story resonates with, or speaks to, the bigger picture of development trends. Finally, I highlight the importance of local knowledge based on story-sharing as an effective resource in enabling individuals and communities of people to be agents of their own change. This approach to social research, I believe, ought to be part of any efforts to understand the nature of, and ways to bring about, development in rural Africa and other similar societies.

Figure 1 is a diagram representing development as experienced and understood from the point of view of the Botoku people. The central, or overarching concern of the study participants, is a perennial quest for a better future. Better future in this context means capacity to bring about changes or improvements in material, social, and spiritual conditions, however defined. Underpinning this perennial quest for a better future is knowledge of history, or past and present interests and aspirations of people, and the sorts of things helping or hindering capacity to fulfill those interests and aspirations. The value of this historical knowledge is certainly intrinsic or important in its own right. But, it also has a strategic value, mainly as guide to future action. Because the quest for a better future forms the basis for the entire model of development, I decided to place it right in the epicentre of the model.

Figure 1: An Integrated Model of Development

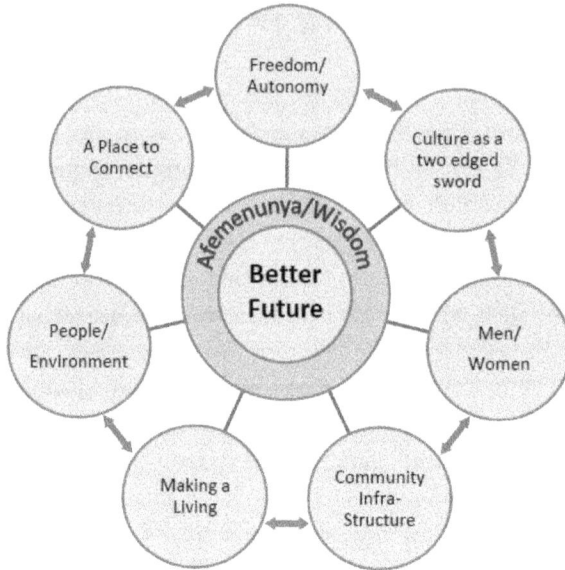

Forming a circle immediately around the epicentre, or the quest for a better future, is *afemenunya* or wisdom from tradition and history. For the Botoku people, life is not so much about whether there are difficulties or not, but how one chooses to understand and deal with them, based on wisdom. Note how *afemenunya*/wisdom is located within the model between the quest for a better future (development) in the centre and the seven main domains or manifestations of development forming the outer circle: 1) freedom and autonomy to be self determining; 2) cultural norms and values; 3) interdependent but fragile relationships between men and women; 4) physical community infrastructure projects such as schools, roads, clinics; 5) making a living through meaningful economic participation; 6) how best to live within the limits of one's environment; and 7) an ancestral home people can connect with physically, emotionally and spiritually, no matter where they are located. This is to distinguish the role of wisdom as virtue and moral guide in helping us make decisions about what is right and what is wrong in our search for a better future, whether material, cultural or spiritual. The other point to make about the model is that it is a holistically integrated

134

approach to understanding human development, encompassing the broad material, social, and spiritual dimensions of the human experience. This interconnectedness is represented by the lines linking each of the seven domains or manifestations of development represented by the outer cycle, as well as linking each domain back to the epicentre of the model. Importantly, theoretical models and frameworks such as this are never fixed in time and space, but always evolving and changing as knowledge accumulates based on day to day experiences and practice.

To possess *afemenunya* is to be a wise person. Some of the attributes of wisdom, frequently cited throughout this book as important in facilitating the quest for a better future, include such human qualities as autonomy, bravery, judgement, forgiveness, empathy, honesty and modesty. They also include the capacity to set boundaries about what is acceptable and what is not; being open to new ideas and able to change with the times; approaching things with balance, courage, dignity and hope; and the desire to make things better for themselves and their children's children (or future generations). Possession of these and other virtues and values makes people wiser, in the sense they are able to discern or judge what is true, right, honourable, or important, depending on context specific situations. In practical terms applying wisdom meant, for example, that traditionally "need" rather than "want" determined how much a person was allowed to take from the available natural environment.

Other dimensions and significance of wisdom are best illustrated through a few additional proverbs and sayings documented throughout this study. The Ewe saying *nunya adido wonye, asi metune o* literally means knowledge itself is as huge as the stem of the baobab tree and hence an individual cannot fully embrace it with their arms. In other words, knowledge is so vast and complex that an individual, no matter how clever, can never fully understand the situation. The real significance of this saying is that as humans, no matter our positions in life, we must be prepared, first and foremost, to accept the limits of our knowledge or understandings. It implies a need for modesty and healthy caution in our claims to knowledge. It also implies the importance of looking at issues from as many angles or points of view as necessary. Another, *koklo ka kolikpo dzi, eno woa tafu nu wokie de,* is literally, the chicken which digs too deep into the dunghill for food risks finding its own mother's thigh bone; meaning, understanding of past injustices and painful memories are important, but dwelling too much on them is of no use to anybody, and may even harm oneself or others.

As a researcher, I was indeed humbled by the extent to which my research informants not only talked about the value of wisdom, but more importantly, the way they approached the whole issue of history, including even the most humiliating and dehumanizing experiences. These experiences included incessant slave raids and wars with their more powerful neighbours, as well as the excesses of colonial rule. These they looked back on with dignity and total acceptance of the situations, responsibility for their actions, and forgiveness with no attempts to blame others for their present predicaments. Given the roles that a sense of historical injustice, both real and imagined, often play as causes of conflict, not only in Africa but in other parts of the world, there's clearly something to learn from the Botoku people's approach to history, and for that matter orientation to life, based on wisdom. It is often said that as humans we do not learn from history. This is definitely not the case with the Botoku experience; for them history is not so much about the chronological and thematic accuracy of specific events, but rather what those events can teach about the human virtues and values that are important to them.

The first manifestation, or domain of development in the model, is freedom, or autonomy to be self-determining of one's own affairs. The most obvious manifestation of the desire to be self determining was the adventurous migratory journey undertaken by the Botoku ancestors out of the Notsie walled city, both to escape Agorkoli's tyrannical rule, as well as to set up their home, hopefully free of enemy attacks. The quest for freedom however is not just about these externally imposed threats to personal freedom and autonomy. It is also about the day to day struggles, by individuals and communities of people, to protect basic human dignity and respect against sometimes coercive and dehumanizing pressures from within. Such would be the case with the development of complex and intricate conflict mediation mechanisms, both to guide relationships between men and women generally, as well as to deal with such dehumanizing crimes as rape and violence against women and children (Chapter 7). It also includes decisions to outlaw trial by ordeal for witchcraft and sorcery accusations. The challenge for researchers, governments and development workers in Ghana and other African communities, is how to draw upon this basic human desire for freedom and autonomy, essential elements in the quest for development, to inform current debates regarding culturally sensitive issues such as how to achieve gender equity, respect for minority groups and sub-groups including ethnic and language diversity and the largely unspoken question of same sex relationships.

The second domain, or manifestation, of development is the role of culture (traditions and customs and associated beliefs) as a two-edged sword. Cultural norms, beliefs and practices provide personal and group identities for people, whether living in their ancestral homes or not. They also provide the values and norms necessary for society to function, such as the expectation that all able-bodied Botoku people, resident or not, will contribute their fair share to the material, social and spiritual improvement of the ancestral home. But culture, as in the case of the trial by ordeal for witchcraft and sorcery accusations, can sometimes undermine the dignity and well-being, not only of individuals, but the community at large.

The evidence from this research suggests that, as development workers and researchers, the question we should be asking about culture, religious beliefs included, is not so much whether it is authentic, invented or appropriate. Rather, the question we should be helping communities with whom we work to ponder or deliberate, is the extent to which a particular custom, tradition or belief system, promotes or undermines the well-being, especially of vulnerable elements of the community, and, if the latter, how the situation might be changed for the better.

Closely related to culture is the need to openly acknowledge that the relationships between men and women are interdependent, but also are fragile. It requires trust and responsibility for both men and women to work together towards building respectful and happy relationships. The most powerful illustration of this is the metaphor of a perforated water pot requiring careful handling by both men and women if the water were to be saved for everyone's benefit. This is why traditionally violence and abuse committed by one man against one woman amounted to no less than a declaration of war by all men against all women, requiring collective rather than individual responsibility and action. In this case men not only respected the freedom of women to collectively withdraw from sexual contact with men, but men also had to ensure that the perpetrator was brought to justice before men and women could resume normal relationships and interactions. Such customs are clearly relevant to the needs and challenges of contemporary Ghana, where rape and violent crimes against women are increasingly treated by the modern judiciary as conflicts between individual victims and the perpetrator.

A fourth domain of development consists of physical community infrastructure projects. These are designed to improve social and economic development of the ancestral village, and would include schools, roads, health services, water, and rural electrification, which was the original object of my study. The role customs and belief systems, such as funeral rites on ancestral lands, play in legitimizing and reproducing the community development tradition is particularly insightful, for at least two reasons.

First, once an issue is identified as a community development priority for the benefit of the entire village, the individual, both resident and non-resident, has little choice but to contribute to the process. Participation in community development, as understood in this particular context, is as much obligatory as it is voluntary. It is obligatory in the sense there are specific sanctions and norms, such as discharge of development obligations as a condition of funeral rites on ancestral lands, to ensure minimum participation. It is voluntary in as far as people often go out of their way to contribute far beyond what may be expected of them. This dual nature of community development expectation in parts of rural Ghana is not properly understood in the relevant literature, which often assumes participation to be mainly voluntary and involving as many people as could be motivated through theoretically sound frameworks, combined with charismatic and skilful leaders.

Second, community development expectations are also a reminder, in the context of globalization and growing individualism, that no "man" is an island. Sometimes people need to be reminded about the strength of collective action. The expectation that all able bodied persons will discharge their development obligations to the native village, and more recently to the church as a condition for relevant funeral rites, continues to remind people, especially young people, of the cooperative nature of morality. This contrasts sharply with wealthy countries such as Australia where, for example, the role of the priest in the church is increasingly reduced to conducting weddings and funeral rituals for people who may have long ceased to be active members of the church. In rural Ghana, even in death, one is called upon to be accountable for one's roles and contributions as member of society.

Another important dimension or domain of development is the ability to make a living through meaningful participation in economic activity. Just as cultural norms and expectations can be harnessed in support of physical communal infrastructure projects, so too the success or otherwise of initiatives designed to promote economic participation, depends on a deep understanding of the relevant local socio-cultural norms and expectations. Of particular relevance here is the need for programs aimed at promoting economic participation, such as development aid income generation initiatives, to strike a balance; that balance being between pooling the resources of communities for the purposes of creating *opportunities* for participation that individuals cannot normally provide on their own, and a need to allow scope for individual control and ownership of the actual process of value creation. This should enable, rather than undermine, enterprise and motivation. Dambisa Moyo (2009), is right in arguing that international aid, no matter how well intended, often has the perverse or negative impact of clouding out financial and social capital, as well as breeding rampant corruption across Africa, and that in the long run, it is sound investment capital that holds the key to Africa's future. For development aid to play meaningful roles in any such transitional phases especially at micro village levels such as Botoku however, research is clearly needed to determine the effectiveness of incorporating traditional notions of responsibility and accountability into such initiatives. An example is the Ewe understanding that the best way to help a person is to help them help themselves. In other words, except in emergencies such as famine situations, we should simply avoid the notion that money is available from somewhere for people to simply access without having to give anything back in return. This type of value system, combined with concepts of social enterprise or using the principles of commercial enterprise towards social objectives, is potentially one way to minimize corruption, dependency and other risks associated with development aid.

Another aspect of economic participation, especially in the context of endemic corruption, is the way social inequality, a recurrent theme throughout this book, can affect the social and moral fabric of society with serious consequences for health and wellbeing, not only for the poor, but also the rich. Evidence from the international literature suggests that higher levels of inequality tend to be associated with more aggression, racial and ethnic conflicts, other forms of prejudice and discrimination, less trust and therefore less social cohesion. Violence and homicide for example, are generally higher where levels of inequality are higher, whereas more egalitarian societies tend to have better community life. Karl Marx vividly described the psychosocial effects of inequality more than a century ago when he said that a house may be large or small; as long as the surrounding houses are equally small, it satisfies all social demands for a dwelling. But if a palace arises beside the little house, the little house shrinks to a hovel and the dweller immediately feels more and more uncomfortable, dissatisfied and cramped within its four walls (Wilkinson, 2000). As social beings, we are constantly reviewing ourselves through other people's lives. It is not surprising we feel insecure and vulnerable in the face of increased inequality, particularly if we perceive ourselves to be losing ground. This is why the Ewe proverb *'ekoe dzie ada, ada dzi valem'* meaning poverty breeds anger and anger breeds violence is highly relevant to contemporary debates about how best to achieve development in Africa. This is not a call for a return to notions of socialist utopia. These are ethical and moral questions requiring open deliberation at all levels of society. More research is clearly needed in order to understand the impact of the massive income inequalities within and across family units in Ghana and other African societies and steps that can be taken to reduce such disparities, at the same time strengthening motivation and respect for hard work and achievement.

Closely related to making a living is how best to live within the limits of one's surrounding environment. This was a constant source of conflict between Botoku people and governments of all persuasion, both colonial and post independent. Although they did not refer to it in environmental terms, commitment to ensuring balance between people and their environment has always been important. This is why the first decisions the new settlers made was to declare all the rivers, water holes, hill tops and caves deities or gods, with stringent customs and taboos regulating the relationships between the people and their environments. This is also why traditionally the concept of need rather than want was preferred as guide to how much we consume or take from the environment. The problem was not so much that the people were against efforts to protect and maintain the ecological environment. Rather, it was the way successive governments have gone about it. The lesson arising from the Botoku experience is clearly the need for governments and policy makers interested in protecting the environment to understand that the key to bringing about change is to respect and value local knowledge as necessary parts of efforts to protect the environment.

The seventh, and final, domain presented in the model is a perception of the ancestral village as a home; a place where, if all else fails, non-residents are able to return to make a living no matter how modest; heal from illness or misfortune; be cared for when they are old or disabled; and ultimately, a place to die or have funeral rituals conducted. The range of creative, if sometimes expensive, ways in which connection to ancestral home was expressed, as in the expense involved in flying bodies from North America or Australia for burial on ancestral lands, suggests a need to rethink the nature of spatial mobility between rural and urban communities.

For the Botoku people, the interests, aspirations and indeed the fortunes of rural and urban dwellers are more intricately intertwined than would appear. The interrelationships between rural dwellers and their urban counterparts, in most parts of Ghana, constitute potentially viable opportunities for more holistic development policies and programs that can make rural living more attractive. These might include incentives for retirees wishing to return to their natal villages, which would also alleviate some of the pressures of urbanization. We need to stop looking at rural-urban migration as a zero sum game and come up with more creative seamless policies and programs to achieve mutual benefits for both urban and rural dwellers alike.

What then is the significance of this integrated approach to understanding development or the quest for a better future? Whether as parents in the family setting; teachers in our educational institutions; health care providers; politicians running the affairs of the state; environmental activists committed to saving the planet; development workers in not-for-profit organizations; or private sector business leaders, a key element of our roles and responsibilities in modern society involves working with people to enhance their capability to take greater control and responsibility over change processes that are characterized by high degrees of complexity, uncertainty and risk as to the most effective courses of action. The focus of the change may vary hugely depending on the particular circumstances and priorities, yet the objective remains the same: how to enable capacity through learning in order to bring about change in a desired direction? Despite the centrality of change in contemporary efforts to improve the human condition, the process is not always properly understood. The assumption made, particularly with regards to people on the margins of societies where deprivation, negativity, poverty and a sense of hopelessness may dominate, is that change will come from outside through knowledge, skills and technical know-how. A classic example is the way Africa has been historically defined through the lens of its problems metaphorically, as the "dark continent," with little interest in digging beyond immediate problems to discover the true essence or humanity of its people. To this day, the dominant image of Africa portrayed by socio-economic statistics and international media remains that of a traumatized people plagued by chronic and debilitating disease, corrupt and incompetent governance systems, and indeed failed states.

The purpose here is not to deny or minimize the enormity of the real challenges and problems confronting Africa; nor to condone unethical behaviour. Too often the power of these images blinds us to crucial facts. These communities, like all human societies, consist by and large of people trying, as best as they can, to go about their daily business of living meaningful lives, however defined. Equally important is that such communities are full of pockets of strength, resiliency, creativity, and innovation, no matter how desperate the situation.

Despite this, the development fraternity for example, continues to assume that best practice models and frameworks such as governance, gender equity and poverty alleviation initiatives, depend on the ingenuity, expertise and generosity of the outsider, despite all sorts of rhetoric about 'bottom up' and 'grassroots' development. This had led to repeated mistakes in 'fixing up' problems for socio-economically vulnerable communities such as rural Africans and for that matter minority indigenous populations in wealthy nations such as Aboriginal Australians, rather than harnessing and supporting those strengths from within.

My research suggests a need to critically re-think our current approaches to development. Rather than premising development initiatives on internationally recognized evidence-based models, development needs to begin, first and foremost, with efforts to investigate and discover how individuals and communities succeed, in spite of difficulties, in improving their material, social and spiritual well-being. The second step is an examination of which internationally proven frameworks can then enhance and enable the existing indigenous or local success stories. It is a case of turning the tables completely upside down. The question we should be asking about development is not what is the problem and how can it be fixed. The question we should be asking is what is working in peoples' lives despite the odds and how can external resources and expertise enhance and enable the things that are already working, despite difficulties.

Beginning from what is working in African societies rather than with problems, despite the severe challenges, makes a lot of sense. The more the things that are working become stronger, the more those involved are empowered or develop greater capacity and confidence to tackle issues that may have appeared intractable at first sight. This inside-out rather than outside-in approach to change is something social scientists interested in

142

organisation development and change have long understood and applied. It is also the essence of the strengths-based and solution-focused approaches for empowering individuals and communities of people to bring about change.

Throughout the course of this research, I was struck by the consistency with which the participants said they were pleasantly surprised by how much Botoku had achieved and how this knowledge or understanding was already motivating them to want to do something to promote further development in the village. Participants in the research discussions, who were not Botoku people, were similarly motivated to want to do something for their own villages. Some contemplated capitalizing on local histories such as this to develop, for example, niche tourism ventures retracing the adventurous migratory journeys from Notsie through to the relevant present day villages and towns. The growing middle classes living away from ancestral homes especially the international diaspora, they believed, would patronize such ventures as a way of connecting their children back to their roots. Others wondered how ideas such as women collectively withdrawing from sexual intercourse with men (Chapter 7) can combine with developments in new media (face book, twitter, emails, and mobile phones) to tackle rape and other interpersonal violence against women. Yet, others imagined a variety of smarter ways in which to transform rural communities in Ghana and similar African countries through education, especially in the context of improved internet communications.

Some saw an opportunity to build the best private boarding schools, comparable to the very best one can find anywhere in the cities and towns across the country. The relative peace and tranquility of rural villages will appeal to the middle classes who are constantly worried about how to protect their children from the risks of urban life (drugs, violent crimes, motor vehicle accidents, endless traffic jams, air pollution) and will patronize such schools in their hundreds and thousands. Profits from fee paying students can then be used to subsidise deserving local students. For others, the best way international aid can help Africa is to spend such resources to provide the highest salary and working conditions for rural teachers. This way the best of the best can be attracted to transform rural schools and more broadly rural communities, as a result of spin-off effects from higher incomes. Above all, Ghanaian and other African governments are encouraged to appreciate the international diaspora, or people living outside Africa, as potentially huge resources to be nurtured and enticed so they can safely invest financially and otherwise in enterprise development while still living outside their own countries.

But the research did not just inspire people to imagine a better future. It also inspired them to act. One of the immediate spin-off actions from the research was the first ever formal community needs analysis carried out voluntarily by a group of seven Botoku people (three residents and four non-residents) in 2008. Despite the relatively impressive achievements of the past, there was a feeling that development to date, as documented in my research, had been mainly ad hoc and opportunistic, without systematic analysis and prioritization of community needs. In response, this highly motivated group of seven, which called itself *Botoku Nede Zo,* literally Botoku to move forward, visited family homes, churches, schools, and organized clan group meetings asking people to identify and rate their priority development concerns. A total of 211 Botoku residents participated in the survey over a period of one week. Education, health and sanitation, as well as governance, and especially the difficulty of finding capable people willing to become clan and paramount chiefs, were the main priority concerns. Two aspects of the findings, with regards to HIV/AIDS and sanitation, are particularly relevant for the present analysis.

With regards to HIV/AIDS, 50% of the respondents did not believe that HIV/AIDS was present in Botoku, 30% said it was, while the other 20% did not know. The main point is not so much about the findings itself or their reliability, but rather the fact the issue of HIV/AIDS became part of the public discourse. Until then it was hard to get development leaders to talk about the subject because of stigma and shame. In fact, the evidence suggests that despite the usual explanations of sorcery, witchcraft and outright denials, families are beginning to rally round those diagnosed with the disease in order to contribute financially towards the relatively expensive treatments. The idea is that the more people are conscious of their past achievements or strengths, the more they can use those strengths as resources to tackle problems that may have been considered unsolvable and hence relegated to the 'too hard' baskets.

With regards to sanitation, as many as 80% said either they did not have, or were not happy with their available toilet facilities. Traditionally, clan groups kept communal pit latrines on the outskirts of the village. But increasingly, individual households are making their own pit latrines in the backyards, while a few people, the emergent middle classes, have put WCs in their houses. This was in a village with little prospect of having access to running water in the foreseeable future. The point to make here is that villages, such as Botoku, can clearly benefit from sound environmentally friendly concepts of sustainable living, especially appropriate technology. In this case the use of composting toilets, rather than uncritically imitating conventional technologies found to be unsustainable even in rich countries, would be beneficial.

But how trustworthy or reliable is the approach to understanding development based on local knowledge and story-sharing as applied in this research? As I finalized the findings of this research, the UN Human Development Program (2010), charged with quantifying and comparing human development in the broadest multi-dimensional forms possible across different countries and over time, fortuitously released its 20th anniversary report. Reading through the report and other World Bank annual assessments of economic performance of poor countries, I was pleasantly surprised by the extent to which the global human development trends and the indicators for Ghana more specifically, confirmed the findings that Botoku was indeed performing reasonably well on some of the manifestations of development.

By all accounts, my micro community project and the human development initiative are worlds apart. The oral history project focuses on the experiences of a single African village, and only a small one at that. It uses the rich traditions of story-telling by the local people themselves with all the minutiae, nuances and juiciness entailed as the methodology, and seeks to understand development from the point of view of the way this particular community experiences, interprets, gives meaning, to and makes sense of development. The UN report, on the other hand, was a worldwide initiative designed to compare human development, as broadly defined as possible, across different societies and cultures. The latter is necessarily a large scale, broad brush bigger picture, highly technical, and quantitative. To compare the two approaches would be like comparing apples and oranges. Perhaps the biblical David and Goliath story best captures the differences in approach between the two. Goliath's might, strength and protective armour is the statistical power and highly technical and sophisticated, expensive computing required to crunch the numbers and compare human development on such a global scale. David represents the modest, small scale approach grounded in the relevant local knowledge traditions. Despite these differences, the two studies are remarkably consistent in their findings. Political freedoms and empowerment, education and health, are clearly areas that Botoku, and for that matter Ghana, have been performing reasonably well over the last 40-50 years, at least since independence from the British.

On the other hand, the two studies also confirm three key domains or areas of development Botoku and Ghana have been performing poorly in, and where attention is urgently needed. The challenge of lifting incomes for the large majority of Ghanaian rural dwellers beyond subsistence production and small scale, or table-top selling, is one. Another is a lack of equity in terms of access to high school education between men and women. This obviously has to do with broader issues of gender equity, respect for ethnic and language diversity and other socially determined inequalities already identified as priority for future research. Environmental hazards, mainly sanitation and air and water pollution, are also major challenges. The point to make here is that, as a global community, we ignore the rich local knowledge traditions, and in this particular case oral history through story-sharing, at our own peril. These are legitimate and vital research methodologies in the global search for the different and creative ways to understand and capture the complexities of human development. What is more, using story-sharing as research methodology has the added advantage of breaking down barriers between people of different social and cultural backgrounds. Story sharing also acts as mirror, so to speak, for participants' self-evaluation of where they have come from, where they are now and how to proceed in the future. They are strategies that can empower and enable individuals and communities of people to be agents of their own change which, in my view, is what development is all about.

I listened to and observed the confidence, hope and positive, future-oriented manner in which my informants imagined a better future for Africa. I could not help but come to the conclusion that for too long, the goals or expectations of development that we set ourselves as Africans, as well as allowing others to set for us, have simply been too low and uninspiring. If we are really interested in a better future for Africa then we have no choice but to engage the broad sections of civil society, the African diaspora included, to help us to raise the development expectations, based on their lived experience as to what is possible and what is not. We cannot continue to keep asking the same old questions about development, but instead need to find new ways of asking old questions.

Instead of asking how to alleviate poverty, we should be asking how to raise incomes and living standards for the large majority of Africa's poor, without, for example, the corresponding wasteful over-consumption patterns and associated rises in the incidence of obesity, as has been the case within rich countries and even the middle classes in Africa. And, as economic conditions improve, how Africa can capitalize on its current robust traditions and norms of family-based support for those in need; to design income support safety nets so as to avoid pockets of intergenerational unemployment, welfare dependency and the associated sense of hopelessness so common with affluent societies? Such bigger picture approaches will require the capacity to think outside the box, so to speak. This way Africa will create new and appropriate knowledge for its own benefit. More than this, such knowledge could hopefully be exported or sold at a premium to other parts of the world, the rich countries included, struggling to deal with over-consumption and diseases of affluence.

The idea here is to reframe Africa's problems as opportunities and indeed, comparative advantages. For example, it is no longer going to be sufficient for those concerned with Africa's development to ask whether it is ethically right or wrong for countries like Ghana to sacrifice scarce resources training doctors, nurses and other skilled workforce including even religious priests, only to lose them in their hundreds and thousands to the affluent nations. The indications are that this trend is bound to accelerate rather than slow down, as it is almost impossible for nation-states to stand in the way of the basic human desire to search for opportunities for self-improvement. Rather, the issue we all need to come to terms with is that in an increasingly interdependent world marked by potentially severe labour shortages in the rich countries, it is in the interests of both poor and the wealthy nations to find mutually beneficial ways of investing through quality education and training in the expected 1 billion additional working age population that is going to become available mainly in Africa, Asia and South America over the next 30 years. As well as averting the potential for social dissatisfaction, unrest and large scale dangerous migration patterns if such labour were left idle, lifting living standards for this 1 billion people through education is the surest way of finally stabilizing and reducing population growth across the entire world. In other words, self interest rather than charity and aid is going to be the key driver of change.

This is where concepts of "need" rather than "want" as guides to consumption identified in this study, combined with evidence from wellbeing research in a wide variety of settings around the world suggesting a need to redefine and strike more sensible balances between how much emphasis we place on economic growth versus human happiness and flourishing, ought to

147

be taken seriously in both rich and poor countries, if we are to come up with models of sustainable living that are mutually beneficial. It is also where I see values-based analytical and reflective story-sharing, as demonstrated in this book and elsewhere with colleagues in the contexts of Aboriginal Australia and Papua New Guinea, as an opportunity to engage different communities of people and cultures through empowering conversations regarding their fears and aspirations of the past, present and the future. This way, civil society is enabled through experiential knowledge and sound and objective research evidence, to be agents of their own change.

But what can the findings from this research contribute to the emerging education for social sustainability field, one of my motivating factors for writing this book? Although the possibilities are many, for the sake of brevity, I will limit myself to three closely related aspects: firstly, the value of creating safe supportive environments for people to share stories, negotiate and mediate disagreements and conflicts, especially over issues such as climate change mitigation and adaptation that are characterised by complexity, uncertainty and risk, and for which there are no straight forward answers as to the best courses of action; secondly, the role of cultural and spiritual identity, or the search for meaning, in facilitating transformative learning and change; and, thirdly, the capacity to reflect and make as transparent as possible the ethical and moral values informing our private and public decision-making processes. The notion of wisdom from tradition as documented throughout this book, I believe, is at the core of contemporary theories and practice of sustainable education such as transformative learning, critical pedagogy, service learning and the whole idea of simultaneously engaging our head, hand and heart towards learning that transforms and enables growth (Scott & Gough, 2004; Sipos, Batisti & Grimm, 2008; Talbot, 2011). Of relevance here is Bent Flyvbjerg's (2001) timely reminder to social scientists that as far as decisions about what is 'good' and 'bad' for society are concerned, *phronesis,* or practical wisdom, ought to *lead* rather than *follow* epistemic science and technical/creative knowledge. This way wisdom can assist individuals, families, communities of people and importantly government policies as to how best to put humanity's phenomenal scientific, technical and creative knowledge and achievements to ethical use. That our recent intellectual traditions and cultures, and more so western civilisations over the last 100 years have done precisely the opposite by elevating and conflating quantifiable scientific evidence with the ethics of what is right and wrong for society clearly amounts to putting the knowledge

148

cart before the knowledge horse. Students, teachers, researchers and others interested in education for sustainability broadly, and not just the social dimensions, need to better understand what makes individuals, a society and its institutions wise in character. Issues such as the contemporary attributes and capacities, as well as the sorts of choices and decisions that would distinguish those possessing wisdom from those without them, require further attention. The attributes of wisdom captured in this book and elsewhere with colleagues in the contexts of Aboriginal Australian empowerment and wellbeing research as well as the emerging human wellbeing, happiness and flourishing research more broadly, constitute one starting point.

Chapter 11

Conclusion

In this concluding chapter, I return to the questions posed at the beginning of this book: what at all is wrong with Africa and why is it that nothing good comes out of Africa?

The main point I wish to make in summation is that, whether as Africans living in Africa, Africans living overseas (the diaspora), or non-Africans concerned with development in Africa, the first thing we all need to understand is that Africa is not at all different from any other human society, past or present. Like all human societies, good things come out of Africa, just as bad things also come out of Africa. It all depends on what we decide to look for. If we look for tragedy, there is no denying the fact that Africa, historically, has had more than its fair share of tragedies. If we look for good news stories, again Africa, contrary to what many might think, is also full of good news stories.

In this book, I deliberately set out to create space or opportunity for one particular community of Africans to tell and share their own stories of development. This is because, despite the vast amount of writings on how to promote development in Africa, the voice of ordinary Africans has been conspicuously absent.

My intention was not to deny or minimize all the real, and often intractable problems, currently confronting Africa. My intention, rather, was to show that in the midst of all the problems of Africa there have been, and will always be, pockets of alternative good news stories. These, often told by people experiencing the problems first hand, are largely from positions of strength in the face of adversity, rather than victimhood.

For the Botoku people, development is all about the quest for a better future. There are two closely related dimensions to the quest for a better future. One is freedom and autonomy to be able to look for, and take advantage of opportunities to achieve a better future for themselves and their offspring or future generation. This is why from time immemorial, travel has always been an integral part of their being. It is therefore not surprising at all that an estimated two-thirds of the Botoku citizens live outside the ancestral rural home. Travel in search of opportunity to better one-self certainly increased with rapid urbanization in the last 40 years or so. But it is wrong to consider recent rural-urban migration as an entirely new phenomenon. It is more appropriate to understand such recent developments as a stage, albeit an accelerated one, in a long process in their search for opportunities to attain a better future. The other dimension of the search for a better future is the knowledge that there is always an ancestral home, or place with which they can connect or identify with, no matter where the search for opportunities to better themselves takes them. For some this connection may be physical as in a place to live, visit, return in old age to die, or to have funeral rituals conducted, no matter where they died. For others, this connection may simply be a state of mind; emotional and spiritual.

There is much to be learned from this. First, in the context of so-called global village it is critical to invest in quality education and training for all, to give people, especially young people, the necessary skills and world views required for them to function or fit in, so to speak, anywhere the search for opportunity takes them. Second, the propensity to chase after opportunities to improve is part of what makes us human. Governments and policy-makers need to understand that they must accept this natural tendency for people to want to travel in search of opportunity as an asset and work out how to best regulate and control the process. It is futile trying to prevent it. Third, development policies need to support people, no matter where they live, to connect with their ancestral roots if they so desire, because this promotes self-identity, purpose and well-being. Finally, as humans, oral histories through story-sharing are powerful mechanisms to restore indigenous cultures and traditions of wisdom, what Aristotle called *phronesis* or practical wisdom, into our interpersonal and social relationships, as well as to the way we relate to the physical environments around us.

To develop real appreciation for the significance of the stories presented in this book, development workers and researchers must be prepared to invest the necessary time and energy required, to listen deeply and to understand the ways in which people use such stories to make sense of their own situation, no matter how dire. Specifically, I hope to have shown that Botoku, like other Ghanaian and indeed African rural communities, has good news stories about the enigma, or the complex and difficult to pinpoint concept, of development. What is more important, is the idea that there are things about development that some of these African villages might well be able to teach the rest of the world, including the rich countries, in the same way there are so many things villages such as Botoku will no doubt continue to learn from the rest of the world.

The starting point for understanding, and hence promoting development, or the quest for a better future for the Botoku people, is going back in time to dig deep into history. This recent history began at least some 300-400 years ago when their ancestors were believed to have escaped as part of a broader Ewe exodus out of the Notsie walled-city in present day Togo. Their main motivation was to gain freedom from servitude and tyrannical rule. This was at the time when demand for slaves, both within the emergent African feudal structures and institutions, as well as for export, especially to the Americas, meant that powerful chieftains increasingly raided smaller vulnerable groups. Perhaps more vicious and sinister was the fact that corrupt and greedy chieftains were even prepared to use any minor transgressions as a flimsy excuse to sell their own people into slavery. The wars that the migrating ancestors fought along the way in their search for a new home, their permanent settlement in present day Botoku, the frequent threats to the peace and stability of the settlement, were all legitimate and necessary parts of this history.

So too were the contradictions brought about by European colonial rules, first imposed on the region by the Germans following the 1885 Berlin Conference, and later after their defeat in the First World War, by the British under the UN mandate. The establishment of colonial rules contributed to gradual reductions in the internecine wars and slave raids, thereby fostering some resemblance of stable macro political climates. But, ironically, the same colonial rule, both German and British, by their very nature of being externally imposed authoritarian regimes with little regard for the interests and aspirations of the ruled, necessarily brought with them their own threats to personal freedoms, peace and stability. For the Botoku people, this manifested in the chiefs and elders, and indeed able-bodied citizens, having to literally and figuratively vote with their feet by frequently taking to the bush at the sight of visiting colonial officials, in order to escape the routine demand for forced labour and *lampo* (taxes) and the associated dehumanizing and instant punishments such as flogging, meted out to those failing to comply.

With Ghana's independence from the British in 1957, the authoritarian pressures of the colonial era rapidly faded away, but again only to be quickly replaced by other new and overt pressures to personal liberties and freedoms. For the Botoku people, and indeed other Ewe villages and towns at the time, Kwame Nkrumah's draconian detention without trial legislation against those professing a united Ewe, designed presumably to protect the territorial integrity of the new independent Ghana, literally drove scores and hundreds of Ewe chiefs and unification sympathizers into self-imposed exile in Togo. In a twist of irony, these late 1950s refugees thus completed what amounted to a full political cycle back to where it all started several centuries ago, at the very Notsie and its environs (Togo is only a tiny country) where their forebears had dramatically escaped in search of freedom and autonomy. Luckily, and hopefully, it was the last time a Botoku person or people would pack their bags to physically escape the village because of overt external pressures and threats to personal and political freedoms and autonomy.

Since then, post independent Ghanaian governments, notwithstanding their ideological orientations, became increasingly relatively attuned to the needs of rural communities. This, combined with stable community level governance based on the traditional chieftaincy and an emergent educated development leadership, enabled meaningful and significant development, even if modest by international standards, to occur. What clearly emerges from this history is a sombre reminder for those interested in Africa's development that, until as recently as the last 50 years or so in the entire recent 300-400 year history, Botoku and similar West African communities, had rarely known or experienced one of the fundamental ingredients of development, namely, freedom and autonomy to pursue one's interests and aspirations without having to constantly look over their shoulders. What makes some African villages and countries achieve relative peace and stability despite often brutal histories of conflicts and abuse of power, while others are still bogged down from time to time by conflict and violence, and what can be done to improve the situation, are clearly important starting questions in any efforts to understand and foster development.

For the Botoku people, the value of history is not so much why, when and how particular events occurred. Rather, what is important are the meanings assigned to the events and what they tell us about the types of people they are, or would like to be known for, and the associated values and virtues that helped their aspirations for development. It is from this history that we develop appreciation for *afemenunya,* or wisdom accumulated through decades, if not centuries of tradition. The point here is not so much whether there are problems or difficulties in life but rather, how one understands and approaches such difficulties. Technical and other knowledge types are important and necessary for meaningful development. But wisdom, or capacity to make ethical and moral decisions about what is wrong and what is right in particular circumstances, including the most ethical ways of using technical knowledge itself, clearly elevates wisdom to a central role in the quest for a better future.

The quest for a better future was first and foremost the desire to pursue material, social and spiritual aspirations of life, no matter how defined, in relative peace, free of coercive pressures. This makes freedom and autonomy essential prerequisites and manifestations of development. Other key ingredients and manifestations of development in this particular context include community infrastructure initiatives such as schools, clinics, clean water, roads and electrification; the role of culture as two-edged sword, in the sense that it promotes cohesion, identity and wellbeing but at the same time, if approached uncritically can also undermine the dignity and the rights especially of the vulnerable; how to achieve happy and respectful relationships between men and women, and for that matter people from different cultural backgrounds; interdependent but fragile nature of the relationships between men and women; opportunities to make a living through participation in meaningful economic activity; how to live successfully within the limits of one's environment; and an ancestral home that people can relate or connect to no matter their spatial location. The model of development that emerged from the way the Botoku people experience and talk about their quest for a better future was therefore an interconnected holistic one, encompassing the spiritual, material, social and political domains of life, in many ways similar to the multi-dimension UN human development measures.

Those familiar with development work, especially among traditionally-oriented societies, know how hard it can be to change long held beliefs and practices, even when they clearly violate and undermine the dignity and well-being of what are often vulnerable groups within the society. Issues such as child marriage; the role and position of women; discrimination against minority languages; attitudes towards same-sex relationships; sorcery and witchcraft; female circumcision and honour killing, are a few that come to mind. Contemporary accounts of the ways in which a particular community believe their spiritual and religious practices may have changed over the years is a reminder culture is always changing and evolving. It is also a good reminder that no matter how sensitive and sentimental a contemporary spiritual or cultural practice, people do have choices, and indeed a duty, to change the practice, especially if it is inimical to the rights and well-being of people.

155

The research argues that the way to help Africa develop is to start with its own strengths and build on, or reinvent, such strengths in light of contemporary global challenges. The question we should be asking is not what are the problems and how to solve them but rather, what are the niche areas where Africa is excelling or has comparative advantage, and hence may potentially rival other societies, and how do we reinvent these to solve real problems within Africa, and then hopefully export or sell such ideas to other parts of the world. There are clearly opportunities, not only for Africa to avoid some of the mistakes of unsustainable development of the rich countries, but perhaps more importantly, to generate novel models that can help rich countries solve some of their current intractable problems, such as intergenerational welfare dependency and so-called diseases of affluence, including obesity.

Importantly, the emphasis of rural communities such as Botoku on economic participation through education, training and mobility as key to lifting the poor out of poverty and misery is fundamentally correct. Sadly, though, despite commitment and motivation, it is impossible for whole countries, let alone local communities of people, to go it alone. Modest but significant local gains in the search for a better future, as documented in this book, clearly need to go hand in hand with bold and imaginative global actions. Proposals such as those advocated in *Creating Jobs in a Global Economy 2011-2030,* designed to remove barriers to skilled migration between developed and developing countries, deserve serious policy attention in both rich and poor countries alike. For this to happen, however, it is necessary for us all, whether we live in poor or rich countries, to seriously consider ways in which our current unsustainable "want" based culture of consumption might be replaced by critical but respectful dialogue within oneself and with others about the nature and potential benefits of "need" based consumption. In an interdependent world, labour is increasingly likely to move across national borders in search of opportunity. Cultural and spiritual identity and connection to place such as ancestral homes as documented in this book, is bound to become a valuable resource in assisting people, especially young people, to work out who they are and their life's purpose, no matter where they find themselves.

Today, we live in a world in which we are routinely confronted with the most tragic and ridiculous contradictions. Despite all the advances in science and technology and the potential opportunities they offer to make the world a relatively peaceful, safe and happy place for most people, this is not the reality. While some live by excessive consumption patterns: paying US $25 million for a visit to the moon; indulging in celebrity expenditure patterns; and the incessant desire to get the latest of everything, others live in misery and starvation.

On the basis of such differences as language, religion, gender, sexuality, skin colour and disability, we construct the "other" as the "problem"; an object to fear, despise, treat with contempt, exploit for self-gratification, ignore and sometimes even kill. We are very skilled at criticizing and blaming the powerful other for all our woes, while our own basic inter-personal relationships can leave a lot to be desired.

We are seduced by the constant message that bigger is better; that the latest or newest version of such material items as ghetto-blasters, mobile phones, laptops, clothing, houses, and cars are the things that will make us happy. It does not matter where we live on the globe; these forces challenge and exert significant influences on the choices we make. This in a world where scientific evidence tells us there are not only limits to our natural resource reserves, but that the universe can only take so much of the ever increasing waste that comes with the concept that bigger or newer is better.

Yet, decisions about what is good and what is bad for society, which the ancient Greeks and many indigenous knowledge traditions believed ought to be guided by wisdom, is today reduced to image driven opinion polls. It is of little surprise that, despite all our scientific and technological advances, many people today, irrespective of whether they live in poor or rich countries, are confused as to our purpose in this life. This is where I see a potential role for *afemenunya,* or wisdom, in helping individuals, communities of people, our institutions, and social structures such as schools, universities, government agencies, and the private sectors, to become wiser in working out what is and isn't really important, and by what criteria.

One way to do this is to draw upon rich local traditions of story sharing to create safe and respectful space for communities of people of diverse social and cultural backgrounds to talk about their development aspirations and interests, the sorts of things that enabled or stood in the way of such aspirations in the past, and the implications for such lessons for the future. Questions such as: where are we going as a family, where are we going as a community or society, where are we going with the safety and welfare of children, with alcohol and drugs, with violence, with stress at the workplace, where are we going with our beliefs and attitudes about climate change mitigation and adaptation, HIV/AIDS, about gender relationships, corruption, witchcraft and sorcery, where are we going with income inequality, does my current position in the inequality hierarchy make me part of the problem or part of the solution, where are these beliefs and attitudes coming from, who benefits and who loses, and by what mechanisms of power, is the direction we are taking desirable, what can I/we do to improve the situation and with what possible consequences, are a good way to start.

Chapter References

Chapter 1
Ashley, C., & Maxwell, S. (2001). Rethinking rural development. *Development Policy Review, 19*(4), 95-425.

ARUP. (2008). Drivers of change: Urbanisation, London: ARUP.

Keyes, C. L. M. (2005). Mental illness and/or mental health? Investigating axioms of the complete state model of health. *Journal of Consulting and Clinical Psychology, 73*, 539-555.

United Nations Human Development Report. (2008). New York: United Nations.

United Nations The Millennium Development Goals Report (2011). New York: United Nations.

Chapter 2
United Nations Human Development Report. (2010). New York: United Nations.

Chapter 3:
Bruner, J. (1990). *Acts of meaning.* Massachusetts: Harvard University Press.

Chapter 4:
Dzobo, N. K. (1992). Knowledge and truth: Ewe and Akan Conceptions. In K. Wiredu & K. Gyekye (Eds.), *Person and community: Ghanaian philosophical studies, cultural heritage and contemporary change II,* 1, (pp. 73-84). Washington, DC: Council for Research in Values and Philosophy.

Flyvbjerg, B. (2001). *Making social science matter: Why social inquiry fails and how it can succeed again.* Cambridge: Cambridge University Press.

Lawrance, B. (Ed.). (2005). *The Ewe of Togo and Benin.* Accra: Woeli Publishing Services.

Patterson, K. D. (1981). The influenza epidemic of 1918-1919 in the Gold Coast. *Journal of African History, 22,* 485-502.

Perbi, A. A. (2007). *A history of the Indigenous slavery in Ghana from the 15th to the 19th century.* Accra: Sub-Saharan Publishers.

Schram, S. S., & Caterino, B. (Eds.). (2006). *Making political science matter* (pp. 33-55). New York and London: New York University Press.

Tsey, K., (2010). Making social science matter?: Case studies from community development and empowerment education research in rural Ghana and Aboriginal Australia. *Asian Social Science, 6*(1), 3-12.

Chapter 5:
Government of the Gold Coast. (1908). Annual report of Transport Department, Accra: Government Printer.
Hill, P. (1963). *The migrant cocoa farmers of southern Ghana*. Cambridge: University Press.
Hopkins, A. G. (1973). *An economic history of West Africa*, London: Longman.
Tsey, K., & Short, S. D. (1995). From headloading to the Iron Horse: The unequal health consequences of railway construction and expansion in the Gold Coast (Ghana). *Social Science and Medicine, 40*(5), 613-621.

Chapter 6:
Chambers, R. (Ed.). (1970). *The Volta resettlement experience*. London: Pall Mall Press.

Chapter 8:
Moyo, D. (2009). *Dead aid: Why AID is not working and how there is another way for Africa*. London: Allen Lane.
WHO Commission on Social Determinants of Health. (2008). Closing the gap in a generation: Health equity through action on the social determinants of health. Geneva: World Health Organization.

Chapter 10
Flyvbjerg, B. (2001). *Making social science matter: Why social inquiry fails and how it can succeed again*. Cambridge: Cambridge University Press.
Moyo, D. (2009). *Dead aid: Why AID is not working and how there is another way for Africa*. London: Allen Lane.
Scott, W., & Gough, S. (2004). Sustainable development and learning: Framing the issues. London: RoutledgeFalmer.
Sipos, Y., Batisti, B., & Grimm, K. (2008). Achieving transformative sustainability learning: Engaging head, hands and heart. *International Journal of Sustainability in Higher Education, 9*(1), 68-86.
Talbot, P. (2011). Aha Malawi! Envisioning field experiences that nurture cultural competencies for pre-service teachers. *International Journal of Multicultural Education, 13*(1), 1-16.

United Nations Human Development Report. (2010). New York: United Nations.

Wilkinson, R. G. (2000). *Mind the gap: Hierarchies, health and human evolution.* New Haven: Yale University Press.

Bibliography

Adams, R. H., & Page, J. (2005). Do international migration and remittances reduce poverty in developing countries?. *World Development, 33*(10), 1645-69. doi:10.1016/j.worlddev.2005.05.004

Argyle, M. (1998). Sources of satisfaction. In I. Christie & L. Nash (Eds.), *The good life*. London: Demos Collection.

Arslanalp, S., & Henry, P. B. (2004). Helping the poor help themselves: Debt relief or aid?. *NBER Working Paper No. 10230*, January 2004.

Arslanalp, S., & Henry, P. B. (2006). Policy watch: Debt relief. *Journal of Economic Perspectives, 20*(1), 207-20.

ARUP. (2008). *Drivers of change: Urbanisation*. London: ARUP.

Ashley, C., & Maxwell, S. (2001). Rethinking rural development. *Development Policy Review, 19*(4), 395-425.

Azam, J., & Flore, G. (2006). Migrant remittances and economic development in Africa: A review of evidence. *Journal of African Economies, 15*(2), 426-62.

Bainbridge, R., McCalman, J., Tsey, K., & Brown, C. (2011). Inside-out approaches to promoting Aboriginal Australian wellbeing: Evidence from a decade of community-based participatory research. *The International Journal of Health, Wellness and Society, 1*(2), 13-28.

Black, A. W. (2004). The quest for sustainable, healthy communities. *Australian Journal of Environmental Education, 21*(1), 33-44.

Bok, D. (2010). *The politics of happiness: What government can learn from the new research on well-being*. Princeton and Oxford: Princeton University Press.

Bolden, R. (2009). African leadership: Surfacing new understandings through leadership development. *International Journal of Cross Cultural Management, 9*(1), 69-85.

BRAC. (n.d.). *Ultra poor programme in Bangladesh*. Retrieved from http://brac.net

Bruner, J. (1990). *Acts of meaning*. Massachusetts: Harvard University Press.

Campfens, H. (1997). *Community development around the world: Practice, theory, research, training*. Toronto: University of Toronto Press.

Cavaye, J. (2001). Rural community development - new challenges and enduring dilemmas. *The Journal of Regional Policy Analysis, 31*(2), 109-124.

Chambers, R. (1970). *The Volta resettlement experience*. London: Pall Mall Press.

Collier, P. (2007). *The bottom billion: Why the poorest countries are failing and what can be done about it*. Oxford: Oxford University Press.

Collier, P., & Hoeffler, A. (2002). *Greed and grievance in civil war*. Centre for the Study of African Economies, Department of Economics, Oxford: Oxford University, WPS 2000-18. Retrieved from http://www.csae.ox.ac.uk/workingpapers/pdfs/2002-01text.pdf

Diamond, J. (1998). *Guns, germs and steel: A short history of everybody for the last 13,000 years*. New York: Vintage Press.

Dzobo, N. K. (1992). Knowledge and truth: Ewe and Akan conceptions. In K. Wiredu & K. Gyekye (Eds.), *Person and community, Ghanaian philosophical studies, cultural heritage and contemporary change* II (pp. 73-84). Washington, DC: Council for Research in Values and Philosophy.

Flyvbjerg, B. (2001). *Making social science matter: Why social inquiry fails and how it can succeed again*. Cambridge: Cambridge University Press.

Frey, B., & Stutzer, A. (2002). *Happiness and economics*. Princeton and Oxford: Princeton University Press.

Government of the Gold Coast. (1908). *Annual report of Transport Department*. Accra: Government Printer.

Hamilton, C. (2003). *The growth fetish*. Crows Nest: Allen and Unwin.

Headey, A., & Wearing, B. (1998). Who enjoys life and why? Measuring subjective wellbeing. In R. Eckersly (Ed.), *Measuring progress: Is life getting better?* Collingwood: CSIRO.

Hill, P. (1963). *The migrant cocoa farmers of southern Ghana*. Cambridge: Cambridge University Press.

Hobsbawm, E., & Ranger, T. (2003). *The invention of tradition*. Cambridge: Cambridge University Press.

Hopkins, A. G. (1973). *An economic history of West Africa*. London: Longman.

International Fund for Agricultural Development [IFAD]. (2011). *Rural poverty report 2011 – New realities, new challenges: new opportunities for tomorrow's generation*. Rome: IFAD.

Kasser, T., & Ryan, R. (1993). A dark side of the American dream: Correlates of financial success as a central life aspiration. *Journal of Personality and Social Psychology, 63*, 410-422.

Keyes C. L. M. (2005). Mental illness and/or mental health? Investigating axioms of the complete state model of health. *Journal of Consulting and Clinical Psychology, 73*, 539-555.

Kovach, M. (2009). *Indigenous methodologies. Characteristics, conversations, and contexts*. Toronto: University of Toronto Press.

Labonte R. (2007). Globalization and health promotion: The evidence challenge. In D. V. McQueen & C. Jones (Eds.), *Global perspectives on health promotion effectiveness.* New York: Springer/International Union for Health Promotion and Education.

Laurence, W. F. (2001). Future shock: Forecasting a grim fate for earth. *Trends in Ecology and Evolution, 16*(10), 531-533.

Lawrance, B. (Ed.) (2005). *The Ewe of Togo and Benin.* Accra: Woeli Publishing Services.

McCalman, J., Tsey, K., Kitau, R., & McGinty, S. (in press). "Bringing us back to our origin": Adapting and transferring an Indigenous Australian values-based leadership capacity building course for community empowerment in Papua New Guinea. *Community Development Journal.*

McCalman, J., Tsey, K., Wenitong, M., Wilson, A., McEwan, A., Cadet James, Y., & Whiteside, M. (2010). Indigenous men's support groups and social and emotional wellbeing: a meta-synthesis of the evidence. *Australian Journal of Primary Health, 16*, 159-166.

Minkler, M., & Wallerstein, N. (2008). *Community based participatory research for health.* San Francisco: Jossey Bass.

Mishkin, F. S. (2006). *The next great globalization: How disadvantaged nations can harness their financial systems to get rich.* New Jersey, Princeton University Press.

Moyo, D. (2009). *Dead aid: Why AID is not working and how there is another way for Africa.* London: Allen Lane.

Pascale, R. R., & Stenin, J. (2006). Your company's secrete change agents. *Harvard Business Review, May,* 73-81.

Patterson, K. D. (1981). The influenza epidemic of 1918-1919 in the Gold Coast. *Journal of African History, 22,* 485-502.

Pearson, N. (2006). *Arthur Mills Oration.* Royal College of Physicians, 7 May 2006.

Perbi, A. A. (2007). *A history of the Indigenous slavery in Ghana from the 15th to the 19th century.* Accra: Sub-Saharan Publishers.

Pusey, M. (1998). Incomes, standards of living and quality of life. In R. Eckersly (Ed.), *Measuring progress: Is life getting better?* Collingwood: CSIRO.

Sachs, J. (2005). *The end of poverty: Economic possibilities for our time.* London: Penguin.

Schmidt-Hergeth, A., & Tsey, K. (1996). Unabhangige initiativen der stadtischen elite: Development Associations in Ghana. *Zeitschrift Der Arbeitsgemeinschaft Entwicklungsethnologie E. V.,* Heft 2, 5 Jg, 34-43.

165

Schram, S. S. & Caterino, B. (Eds.) (2006). *Making political science matter* (pp. 33-55). New York and London: New York University Press.

Scoones, I. (1998) *Sustainable rural livlihoods: A framework for analysis.* IDS Working Paper 72. Brighton, UK: Institute of Development Studies.

Scott, W. & Gough, S. (2004). *Sustainable development and learning: Framing the issues.* London: RoutledgeFalmer.

Sipos, Y., Batisti, B., & Grimm, K. (2008). Achieving transformative sustainability learning: Engaging head, hands and heart. *International Journal of Sustainability in Higher Education, 9*(1): 68-86.

Talbot, P. (2011). Aha Malawi! Envisioning field experiences that nurture cultural competencies for pre-service teachers. *International Journal of Multicultural Education, 13*(1), 1-16.

Tanner, L., (2011). *Sideshows: Dumbing down democracy.* Carlton North, Vic: Scribe Australia.

Thomas, S. (2008). Urbanization as a driver of change. *The Arup Journal, 1*, 58-67.

Tsey, K. (1997). Aboriginal self-determination, education and health: Towards a more radical attitude towards Aboriginal education. *Australian and New Zealand Journal of Public Health, 21*(1), 77-83.

Tsey, K., (2010). Making social science matter?: Case studies from community development and empowerment education research in rural Ghana and Aboriginal Australia. *Asian Social Science, 6*(1), 3-12.

Tsey, K. (2001). Traditional healers and mental health care in rural Ghana. *Australasian Review of African Studies, 23*(2), 20-30.

Tsey, K. (1997). Traditional medicine in Ghana: A public policy analysis. *Social Science and Medicine, 45*(7), 1065-1074.

Tsey, K., Schmidt-Hergeth, A., & Lubrani, O. (1995). The role of Indigenous social organisations in rural development in West Africa: Some lessons for NGOs. *Development Bulletin, 35*, 47-50.

Tsey, K., & Short, S. D. (1995). From headloading to the Iron Horse: The unequal health consequences of railway construction and expansion in the Gold Coast (Ghana). *Social Science and Medicine, 40*(5), 613-621.

Tsey, K., Patterson, D., Whiteside, M., Baird, L., & Baird, B. (2002). Indigenous men taking their rightful place in society? A preliminary analysis of a participatory action research process with Yarrabah Men's Health Group. *Australian Journal of Rural Health, 10*(6), 278-284.

Tsey, K., Whiteside, M., Cadet-James, Y., Haswell, M., Bainbridge, R., & Wilson A. (2009). Empowerment and Indigenous Australian health: A synthesis of findings from family wellbeing formative research. *Health and Social Care in the Community, 18*(2), 169-179.

UNESCO. (2002). *United Nations Decade of Education for Sustainable Development (2005-2014): International Implementation Scheme.* Paris: UNESCO.

United Nations. (2011). *The Millennium Development Goals Report.* New York: United Nations.

United Nations Commission on Environment and Development [UNCED]. (1987). *Brundtland Report: Our common future.* Oxford: Oxford University Press.

United Nations Department of Economic and Social Affairs [DESA]. (2008). *Trends in sustainable development: 2008-2009.* New York: United Nations.

United Nations Department of Economic & Social Affairs [DESA]. (2009). *World urbanization prospects: The 2009 revision highlights.* New York: United Nations.

United Nations Development Program. (2008). *Human Development Report 2007/8: Fighting climate change: Human solidarity in a divided world.* New York: United Nations.

United Nations Development Program. (2010). *The Human Development Report 2010: The Real Wealth of Nations: Pathways to Human Development.* New York: United Nations.

Wallerstein, N. (2006). *What is the evidence on effectiveness of empowerment to improve health?* Retrieved from http://www.euro.who.int/__data/assets/pdf_file/0010/.../E88086.pdf

Whiteside, M., Tsey, K., & Earles, W. (2011). Locating empowerment in the context of Indigenous Australia. *Australian Social Work, 64*(1), 113-129.

WHO Commission on Social Determinants of Health. (2008). *Closing the gap in a generation: Health equity through action on the social determinants of health.* Geneva: World Health Organization.

Wilkinson, R. G. (2000). *Mind the gap: Hierarchies, health and human evolution.* New Haven: Yale University Press.

World Commission on Environment and Development. (1987). *The Brundtland Commission.* Oxford: Oxford University Press.

www.ingramcontent.com/pod-product-compliance
Lightning Source LLC
Chambersburg PA
CBHW022320280326
41932CB00010B/1166